DATE		
NOV 29 91		
NOV 06 92		

DiRTY POLITICS

FROM 1776 TO WATERGATE

CONFRONTATION—Politics and Protest

THE GEORGE WALLACE MYTH

KING OF THE COURTROOM

THE MAKING OF A SLUM

PAYOFF—The Role of
Organized Crime in American Politics

THE SECOND MAN—The Changing
Role of the Vice Presidency

THE SECRET SERVICE STORY

UNDER 21: A Young People's
Guide to Legal Rights

VESCO—The Infernal
Money-Making Machine

WE SHALL OVERCOME

WITCH HUNT—The Underside
of American Democracy

DETECTIVES OF THE SKY

DiRTY POLITICS

FROM 1776 TO WATERGATE

MICHAEL DORMAN

DELACORTE PRESS/NEW YORK

Published by
Delacorte Press
1 Dag Hammarskjold Plaza
New York, N.Y. 10017

Manufactured in the United States of America
First printing

Designed by JoAnne Bonnell

Library of Congress Cataloging in Publication Data

Dorman, Michael.
 Dirty politics.

 Bibliography: p. 285
 Includes index.
 SUMMARY: Details examples of dirty politics
practiced throughout the nation's history including
ballot fraud, election rigging, spying, sabotage, and
smear campaigns. Discusses Watergate and moves for
reform.
  1. Corruption (in politics)—United States—History
—Juvenile literature. [1. Corruption (in politics)
2. United States—Politics and government] I. Title.
JK2249.D67   320.9'73   77-86319
ISBN 0-440-01949-4

This book is dedicated to the memory of J. Neal Matthews, a diligent law enforcement officer who spent much of his life trying to eliminate dirty politics in Texas, and to Judge Joe Ingraham of the U.S. Fifth Circuit Court of Appeals, who first gave me the notion that the word "politics" was not dirty—that, in its broadest sense, it referred to service toward "the public good."

CONTENTS

INTRODUCTION

Gordon Strachan was a bright, handsome young lawyer who had risen to a position of prominence and responsibility far beyond his expectations. By 1972 he was an important political aide to President Richard M. Nixon and served as the White House liaison man with the committee managing the president's re-election campaign. A future of unlimited horizons seemed to lie before him.

But then, along with numerous others, Strachan was caught up in the furor the world has come to know as the Watergate scandal. He left the White House in disgrace. Eventually, he was indicted on charges of conspiracy, obstruction of justice, and making false statements to a grand jury investigating the Watergate cover-up.

INTRODUCTION

In 1973, while testifying before a Senate committee looking into the scandal, Strachan was asked what advice he would give to young people contemplating careers in politics and government. After reflecting for a moment, he replied: "My advice would be to stay away."

Strachan's sad, disillusioned response was understandable. At the time, the public was witnessing exposure of the most glaring breaches of political ethics in the nation's history. Investigation had revealed not only that agents of the president's re-election organization had burglarized and wiretapped their opponents' national headquarters, but also that Nixon campaign operatives had participated in a seemingly endless chain of other political dirty tricks.

Spies had been planted in the campaign organizations of opposition Democratic candidates. Forged letters had been mailed on stolen copies of the opposing candidates' stationery, making fraudulent statements designed to create confusion and dissension in the Democratic ranks. Scurrilous smear literature—falsely accusing various Democratic presidential aspirants of everything from mental instability to bizarre sexual behavior—had been widely distributed. Nixon's agents had hired young men and women to dress in disreputable-looking clothes and pose as demonstrators supporting Democratic candidates. Other Republican operatives, pretending to be Democratic campaign workers, had awakened sleeping voters with annoying late-night telephone calls.

In further attempts to antagonize voters against the Democrats, Republican agents had sent out letters inviting citizens to attend dinners and parties supposedly being given by Democratic candidates—promising that "free food and alcoholic beverages" would be served. No such functions had actually been planned by the Democrats, and the people who responded to the phony invitations were naturally incensed. On other occasions, Nixon's spies had placed fraudulent orders for large quantities of food and beverages to be sent and billed to the headquarters of Democratic candidates. The Democrats had no use for such provisions and were, of course, embarrassed by their arrival. The list of dirty tricks went on and on, as will be described later in this book. Perhaps the strangest of all was the Republicans' hiring of a young woman to run naked in front of a Democratic candidate's headquarters, proclaiming her love for the candidate.

Although the events associated with the Watergate scandal represented an all-time low in American political ethics, dirty politics have been woven into the fabric of the nation's history virtually since the founding of the country. As this book will show, numerous elections for local, state, and national offices have been stolen through outright ballot frauds. Other elections have been rigged by such means as intimidation of voters and gerrymandering (manipulation of election-district boundaries to favor one candidate or party). Long before Watergate, politicians had resorted to planting spies in their opponents' campaign organizations. Smear campaigns, use of forged or fraudulent documents, and deliberate distortion of a candidate's record or program have been staples of American political life for generations.

This book will spell out in detail some of the most flagrant examples of dirty politics practiced throughout the nation's history. But it is not my intention to influence young readers to follow Gordon Strachan's advice to "stay away" from careers in politics and government. On the contrary, I believe that well-informed young people—outraged by the dirty politics of past and present—offer the best hope of raising ethical standards of future election campaigns.

Several studies conducted in the aftermath of Watergate revealed that many students had become extremely cynical about politics. They assumed that most political and governmental leaders were crooked and concerned solely with their own ambitions. I find these assumptions disturbing and fallacious. I have spent much of my adult life reporting and writing about politicians, ranging from local ward heelers to presidents of the United States. Despite their shortcomings, I have found most of them to be honest, dedicated public servants. I feel strongly that the few who abuse their political influence should be exposed and driven from their positions of power. But I feel equally that the sins of those few should not poison the public's attitude toward all public figures.

In describing the dirty politics of past and present, I hope to alert readers to the challenges facing those who seek genuine reform. Along with examples of dirty politics, I will describe means of reforming the American political process. Some have been adopted, but many more are the subject of intense debate. It is my earnest hope that young people who read the book—far from being turned off by politics—will decide to enlist in a campaign to elevate the level of political ethics.

Sir Walter Scott wrote of "the open truth and fiery vehemence of youth." That open truth and fiery vehemence, if channeled into a drive to clean up campaign practices, could serve as the perfect antidote to the dirty politics tearing at the very fabric of American society.

MICHAEL DORMAN
Dix Hills, New York

PART ONE

BALLOT FRAUD AND ELECTION RIGGING

1 THE MIRACLE OF BOX 13

The late President Lyndon Baines Johnson was, among other things, an accomplished narrator of political stories. He often regaled listeners for hours with hilarious yarns about the peculiar brand of politics practiced in his native Texas. One of his favorite tales—in which the joke was on him—went this way:

Once upon a time, on the day after an election, a young Mexican-American boy named Pedro was found crying on the main street of a dusty Texas border town.

"Why are you crying, Pedro?" a man asked him.

"I'm crying for my dead father," Pedro answered.

"But your father has been dead for ten years," the man said. "Why are you crying for him now?"

"I know he's been dead for ten years," Pedro replied. "But yesterday he came back to life to vote for Lyndon Johnson, and he didn't come to see me!"

Numerous observers, in Texas and elsewhere, contend that there is more truth in that story than Lyndon Johnson would ever admit. It is their view that many dead men somehow managed to cast votes for Johnson and that without those fraudulent votes he might never have reached the White House.

In 1948, while serving as a relatively obscure member of the House of Representatives, Johnson entered the race for a vacant Texas seat in the Senate. Four other candidates were campaigning for the position in the Democratic primary. The most prominent among them was Coke Stevenson, who had served two terms as governor of Texas.

Since the Republican party fielded only token candidates in those days in Texas, victory in the Democratic primaries was equivalent to election. In the first primary for the Senate seat, Stevenson led the balloting with 477,077 votes—71,460 more than Johnson, who finished second. But because the remaining votes were divided among the other three candidates, Stevenson failed to win a majority of all ballots cast. Under Texas law, a second (or runoff) primary between Stevenson and Johnson was required to choose the winner of the Senate seat.

During the period between the first and second primaries, Johnson forged a political alliance with a notoriously corrupt southern Texas political boss named George B. Parr. For almost four decades, Parr and his father before him had ruled as virtual feudal barons

4

over a five-county area of oil-rich sagebrush country just north of the Mexican border. Their subjects— thousands of Mexican-Americans—lived in terror of the Parr political machine.

Year after year, the frightened citizens trudged to the polls and voted the straight Parr ticket. This solid bloc of votes, guaranteed to any politician who won Parr's favor, could tip the balance in a close statewide race.

In the runoff, the initial returns from the five counties controlled by Parr gave Johnson 10,547 votes and Stevenson only 368. But Stevenson had run strongly in other parts of the state. When the statewide returns were tabulated, they showed Stevenson defeating Johnson by the razor-thin margin of 112 votes out of a total of almost 1 million cast.

It was then that George Parr reached into his bag of political tricks and produced for Lyndon Johnson what came to be known as "the miracle of Box 13." After all the statewide returns were in and Johnson appeared to be the loser, Parr's election officials in Precinct (Box) 13 in the town of Alice suddenly claimed they had discovered some additional votes that had not previously been counted. Johnson's campaign manager, John Connally (who would later serve as governor of Texas and U.S. secretary of the navy and secretary of the treasury), rushed to Alice to confer with the officials who would count the ballots that had supposedly been found. Former Governor Stevenson— fearing that Parr was in the process of trying to steal the election for Johnson—also hurried to the scene to protect his interests. He took with him two aides,

James Gardner and Kellis Dibrell, who had formerly been FBI agents.

The ballot box from Precinct 13 was put away, purportedly for safekeeping, in a bank vault. The hitch was that the bank, along with almost everything else in the area, was controlled by George Parr.

It was not until six days after the election that Parr's officials submitted their revised tally of the votes from Box 13. They claimed they had found 203 ballots that had not previously been tabulated. Of those, they maintained, 201 had been cast for Johnson and only 2 for Stevenson. Thus, if these supposed ballots were allowed to stand, Johnson would win the primary by 87 votes.

By the time the additional votes were tabulated, a subcommittee of the Texas Democratic Executive Committee—assigned to count and certify the state-wide ballots—had already issued a report declaring Stevenson the winner. But within hours after the sub-committee's declaration of what were assumed to be the final results, Johnson's aides announced that they expected the tabulation of the additional votes from Box 13 to change the outcome.

With the claim that the 201 newly discovered votes for Johnson would give him the victory, the situation in Parr's territory grew tense. Former Governor Stevenson and his aides demanded to see the list of registered voters in Precinct 13 so that they could check whether fraudulent ballots had been cast. Like the supposed ballots, the list of voters had also been locked in the bank vault. Bank officers, some of whom served as election officials for Parr, initially refused to allow

Stevenson's men to see the list. Stevenson's aides had intended to examine it, note the names of the supposed voters, and then check whether such persons actually existed and had voted.

Rumors swept Parr's territory that he and his henchmen were prepared to resort to gunplay, if necessary, to prevent inspection of the voting list. Standing by was his force of *pistolero* sheriff's deputies—heavily armed. Stevenson appealed for help from the state capital in Austin, asking that a force of Texas Rangers be dispatched to the scene to prevent violence and ensure an honest count of the ballots. State officials responded by sending one of the most famous Texas Rangers of all time, Captain Frank Hamer, the man who had tracked down the notorious Bonnie Parker and Clyde Barrow and led the posse that killed them in a blazing Louisiana gun battle.

On the morning after Hamer's arrival, a showdown loomed in Wild West fashion on the street outside the bank. Five of Parr's henchmen, with loaded rifles at the ready, stood ominously across the street from the bank. A dozen others, with pistols conspicuously displayed, formed a semicircle directly in front of the bank. Former Governor Stevenson, fearing Parr's men might try to shoot him and his aides and then claim self-defense, ordered his assistants to take off their coats before approaching the bank—to make clear they were carrying no concealed weapons.

Then, minutes before the bank was scheduled to open, Captain Hamer led Stevenson and his aides toward the bank. He halted a few feet from the semicircle of Parr men, stepped out in front of Stevenson's

7

group, and stood there for a few moments to make sure everyone present recognized him.

In a scene that could have come right out of *High Noon*, Hamer crossed the street and set himself squarely in front of the five riflemen. He pointed his finger to the far end of the street and ordered: "Git!"

The men grumbled and swore for a few seconds, but then obeyed. Hamer next crossed back to the semi-circle of men in front of the bank, surveyed the group silently at first, then barked: "Fall back!" The men cleared a path for Hamer, Stevenson, and his aides to enter the bank.

Tom Donald, a Parr aide who ran the bank and also handled political chores for the local organization, opened the door. Stevenson and his assistants entered, but Hamer would not let the *pistoleros* inside. A short time later, Democratic party officials with responsibility for counting the votes and certifying the election results arrived. One of them, H. L. Adams, demanded that Donald open the bank vault and hand over the election records—since the Democratic party was entitled to serve as custodian of its own primary-race documents. But Donald, acting on George Parr's orders, refused to comply.

"I will permit you to see the voting list, but not to handle it," he said. All he would agree to do was to remove the voting list from the vault, hold it up, and allow the Stevenson men and party officials to view it from across a wide table. Stevenson and his aides began taking down names and immediately spotted several oddities. The persons whose ballots had been belatedly "found" had all signed their names in what seemed to

8

be the identical handwriting. Further, their names appeared in ink that differed in color from all other names on the rolls. As if those facts were not suspicious enough, the "late" voters had somehow managed to cast their ballots in alphabetical order. Since voters usually show up at the polls in haphazard fashion, there seemed no reasonable explanation of why all these citizens would have appeared alphabetically.

After Stevenson and his men had recorded the names of only seventeen voters, however, a telephone rang and was answered by Parr aide Donald. He listened for a minute, then folded the voting list and put it back in the bank vault. "That's all," he said.

Frustrated but determined to plod ahead, Stevenson's men began trying to locate the seventeen persons whose names they had noted. They quickly discovered that four of them could not have voted: they had long been buried in a local cemetery. Another man whose name appeared on the list was found, alive, in a distant Texas city. He denied even being in Parr's county on election day, much less voting there. A local housewife whose name appeared on the list said she had not voted and was not even qualified to vote. After a dogged investigation, Stevenson's aides were unable to find a single person from among the seventeen who had actually voted.

Stevenson and Democratic party officials went into court, charging that Parr had tried to steal the election for Johnson. They asked the courts to take speedy action to prevent such a theft from receiving official sanction. But Johnson and his forces took court action of their own, seeking to certify Johnson as the winner of the election. They accused Texas Ranger Captain Hamer of entering into a conspiracy with Stevenson, various Democratic party officials, and others to have the belatedly "found" votes set aside as fraudulent. And they asked the court to bar any further recount of the votes.

While the rival court actions were pending, the Texas Democratic Executive Committee met in Fort Worth to consider which candidate to certify as the winner. On the first ballot there was a 28-to-28 deadlock between Stevenson and Johnson. A second ballot produced identical results. Then Johnson, his campaign manager, John Connally, and his lawyer, John Cofer, left the room where the meeting was taking place after being promised no additional votes would be taken until they returned. They made arrangements to have a member of the executive committee who had not been present for the prior votes flown to Fort Worth from Amarillo, almost 350 miles away. They did not return to the executive committee meeting until the previously absent member, C. C. Gibson, arrived.

On the next ballot, Gibson voted to certify Johnson as the winner—making the tally 29 to 28. The committee then adjourned its meeting.

Although winning the Democratic primary runoff guaranteed election in Texas, there was still the formality of a general election. The slate certified by the Texas Democratic Executive Committee was ordinarily listed on the ballot for the general election alongside token slates of candidates fielded by the Republicans and minority parties. In many races, the Republicans did not even bother to nominate candidates. But in any event, it would be necessary for the winners of the Democratic nominations to go through the motions of running in general-election campaigns.

Responsibility for printing the official general-election ballots rested with Paul Brown, the Texas secretary of state. At the time of the tight, controversial Democratic Executive Committee meeting, Brown was already facing the deadline for ordering the printing of the ballots. But he could not do so until he knew the outcome of the Johnson-Stevenson contest. Once the committee voted to certify Johnson, Brown ordered the ballots printed with Johnson's name as the official Democratic candidate for the Senate.

Former Governor Stevenson then went into the United States district court in Dallas and filed a new lawsuit seeking to overturn the certification of Johnson as winner by both the Democratic Executive Committee and Secretary of State Brown. Federal Judge T. Whitfield Davidson, in whose court the case was filed, had left Dallas for a weekend of relaxation at a farm he owned near Marshall, Texas. Stevenson drove all night to reach Davidson's farm and asked him to sign a court order preventing, at least temporarily, what the former governor contended was the "theft" of the election.

Judge Davidson, after reading the legal petition presented by Stevenson, agreed to sign the order. It instructed that all election returns and ballots from George Parr's territory be seized, pending court examination. It also barred Secretary of State Brown from printing the general-election ballots until the court examination was completed. A hearing on Stevenson's suit was set for September 21.

11

Immediately after learning of the court order, Secretary of State Brown rushed to the print shop where the ballots were to be produced. He discovered the ballots were about to begin rolling off the presses. At the last moment, he ordered Johnson's name stricken and the ballots printed without a Democratic senatorial candidate listed.

Johnson and his forces soon counterattacked. They tried to persuade a federal appeals court to overturn Davidson's order, but the best they could do was get the appeals court to set a hearing on the matter for October 2—eleven days after Davidson's own hearing. Meanwhile, Davidson appointed a San Antonio attorney, William R. Smith, to conduct an investigation of the purported vote theft for the court. Smith was empowered to go to Parr's territory, take possession of the election records, subpoena witnesses, and gather evidence on all facts related to the runoff election.

Smith lost no time in hurrying to the scene, taking with him federal marshals to help in the investigation. But when they arrived, they discovered that the election records were missing and that the Parr lieutenants whose testimony was wanted had mysteriously gone to Mexico—beyond the reach of the court—on what they claimed was urgent business. The ballot boxes were ultimately found, but all they contained were old newspapers and other trash.

Thus, when the hearing opened on September 21 in Judge Davidson's court, the most critical evidence was absent. The voting list, the ballots, and other election materials were gone. Johnson's team of attorneys, including both John Cofer and a friend of Johnson's

12

named Leon Jaworski (later Watergate special prosecutor), seized the opportunity to claim that Stevenson had no case.

"This plaintiff [Stevenson] lost his race for United States senatorial nominee in a Democratic primary, over which only the regular Democratic officials have jurisdiction," Cofer told Judge Davidson. "This court has no jurisdiction. He [Stevenson] has no civil rights [that are being violated], as pleaded in his petition. He is merely a poor loser."

The judge, however, had little patience for such an argument. Banging his gavel to silence Cofer, Davidson denied his request to throw the case out of court. "This plaintiff, Mr. Stevenson, has duly alleged he has been robbed by fraud of a seat in the United States Senate," the judge said. "Not a shred of evidence has been submitted to disprove his claim. He . . . is entitled to a hearing in open court. And that hearing he shall have. This court will decide on the merits of his petition."

Davidson was wrong. He would not have a chance to conclude his hearing or decide the case on its merits. Lyndon Johnson had retained a noted Washington lawyer, Abe Fortas, to file a petition with U.S. Supreme Court Justice Hugo Black asking him to order Davidson's hearing halted. (Fortas himself would later serve a controversial term on the Supreme Court, on appointment from his former client, then-President Lyndon Johnson.) Fortas's petition to Justice Black did not deal with the merits of the election fraud charges, but merely contended that the issues in the case should be resolved by the Democratic party and not by the federal courts. Justice Black signed an order forbidding Judge Davidson to proceed further with the hearing or otherwise consider Stevenson's case.

Justice Black was empowered to issue such an order on his own because the full Supreme Court was not in session at the time. Theoretically, the full court ultimately could have reversed his ruling. But the effect of the order was to halt Judge Davidson's consideration of the case indefinitely. Since the general election was quickly approaching, there would be little time for the full court to hear arguments and reverse Black's decision in time to allow Stevenson to get his name on the general-election ballot.

Black's court order was flown from Washington to Texas and presented to Judge Davidson by a federal marshal. Davidson reluctantly halted his hearing. "This court has no choice but to submit to the mandate from the Supreme Court, although, in my opinion, Mr. Justice Black has acted hastily and probably illegally," Davidson said.

For all intents, Justice Black's order put an official seal on what many considered Johnson's theft of the Senate seat—with a major assist from George Parr. Time ran out on Stevenson's further efforts to win court consideration of the vote-fraud charges. Secretary of State Brown ordered Johnson's name listed on the ballot as the official Democratic Senate nominee. Johnson then easily swept to victory in the general election.

When he returned to Washington as senator, he had a new nickname—"Landslide Lyndon"—derived from his 87-vote "victory" in the race against Stevenson. Within a few years, he would become the Senate majority leader and be considered the second most

14

powerful man in Washington. Some said he was *the* most powerful, since President Dwight D. Eisenhower was in the White House at the time and was considered by many a weak chief executive. In 1960 Johnson would be elected vice-president on John F. Kennedy's ticket; he would become president upon Kennedy's assassination in 1963 and win his own presidential election a year later.

Thus there is strong reason to speculate that the entire history of the United States might have been radically different if George Parr and his cohorts had not "stolen" the 1948 election for Johnson. If Stevenson had been declared the winner of the senatorial primary, Johnson would have remained in the House for at least several more years. He could not have become Senate majority leader when he did and thus probably would not have been the vice-presidential candidate in 1960. As a result, he would not have become president. He himself observed many times that only a fluke could have put him or anyone else from the South or Southwest in the White House under the political conditions prevailing in the United States in the 1950s and 1960s. Actually, in his case, it took two flukes: the first was the purported "theft" of the Senate election, the second was President Kennedy's assassination.

Meanwhile, George Parr continued delivering lopsided majorities at the polls for his pet candidates. Johnson was a major beneficiary of such election manipulation. Another beneficiary was John Connally, who was elected governor of Texas with help from Parr.

During the early 1970s Parr was indicted on charges

15

of failing to list on his tax returns income of more than $287,000. In March 1974 he was found guilty and sentenced to ten years in prison. He was permitted to remain free on bail while appealing the conviction. In March 1975 the conviction was upheld by a federal appeals court, and government attorneys then filed motions demanding that he surrender and begin serving his sentence. By that time, Parr was seventy-four years old. He had been convicted of other crimes in the past but had served only one prison term.

He was due to appear in court on March 31 for a hearing on the government's surrender demand. When he did not show up, he was listed as a fugitive. Federal marshals were sent to hunt for him, and they found him slumped over the steering wheel of his car in a pasture near his palatial home. He was dead, with a bullet wound in his head. A .45-caliber pistol and an M-14 military rifle lay on the car seat. A local justice of the peace ruled the death a suicide, apparently prompted by Parr's reluctance to serve any more prison time at his advanced age.

By the time of Parr's death, Lyndon Johnson lay in his own grave. There were those who felt the story of the theft of the 1948 Senate election should be buried along with them.

But in mid-1977 a former Parr aide named Luis Salas who had served as an election judge in 1948 admitted to news reporters that he had intentionally certified the fraudulent ballots. Salas said his conscience had been bothering him for years. He also claimed that Johnson had attended a meeting at which the means of stealing the election had been discussed.

16

Old Johnson cronies immediately launched a counter-attack, assailing Salas's credibility. They claimed Johnson had been in Austin at the time Salas reported meeting with him and Parr in southern Texas. The argument tended to obscure the reality of the situation, for it is painfully clear that Johnson and his aides made every possible effort to ensure the election remained stolen after Parr's machine had produced the phony ballots in Box 13.

2 A TRADITION OF PO-LITICAL SKULDUGGERY

Freedom to vote as one pleases is generally considered to be among the most precious rights of an American citizen. Any formal attempt to abolish that right would undoubtedly be doomed to ignominious defeat. Anyone who proposed such abolition could expect to be hooted down (or worse) as an advocate of dictatorial government. Yet almost since the founding of the Republic, prominent men in America have been involved in attempts to thwart the will of the electorate.

The history of presidential politics is replete with allegations of such manipulation. The 1796 election was an early example. At that time, under the Constitution's initial provisions, there was no vote cast by the public at large. Instead, people chosen by each state legislature to serve as members of the electoral

18

college voted directly for president. These individuals were known as presidential electors and were empowered to cast two votes each in the electoral college.

In theory, one of these votes was expected to be cast for president and the other for vice president, but the constitution did not permit an elector to designate the office. Whichever candidate won the most votes in the electoral college became president; the runner-up became vice president.

In the 1796 election, two of the Founding Fathers emerged as leading presidential contenders. John Adams, who had served two terms as George Washington's vice president, was the Federalist candidate. Thomas Jefferson, the anti-Federalist candidate, was his chief opponent. But within the Federalist party Adams faced opposition from a longtime rival, Treasury Secretary Alexander Hamilton. In an attempt to thwart Adams from becoming president, Hamilton contrived a scheme to take advantage of the loophole in the Constitution that prevented electors from designating which candidate they were voting for as president and which as vice president.

Hamilton realized it would be possible, by manipulating votes, to have Thomas Pinckney, the Federalist candidate for vice president, elected as president. Hamilton knew he could control Pinckney, and he reasoned that if he persuaded some electors to vote for Pinckney and to cast their second votes for someone other than Adams, Pinckney would be elected president and Adams vice president—instead of just the opposite.

Accordingly, Hamilton asked the South Carolina electors to vote for their native son, Pinckney, but not for Adams. Meanwhile, he asked electors from northern states to cast ballots for both men. Hamilton's scheme was uncovered, however, by northern Federalists loyal to Adams. They turned the tables on Hamilton—persuading some New England electors to vote for Adams and throw their second vote away on a candidate other than Pinckney.

The result: Adams won the presidency with 71 electoral votes. But Pinckney fell short of the vice-presidency with 59. The second-highest total of electoral votes was won by the opposition presidential candidate, Jefferson, who received 68. Jefferson thus became vice president—presenting the nation with a president from one party and a vice president from another.

Although Adams and Jefferson ultimately became close friends, their early service together was marred by differing philosophies and political styles. In the 1800 presidential election, Jefferson ran against Adams (with Aaron Burr as his running mate). The constitutional imperfection once more came into play, and this time Jefferson and Burr wound up in a tie in the electoral college with 73 votes each. Such a tie, under the Constitution, was to be broken by a vote in the House of Representatives. After much political maneuvering, in which Hamilton again resorted to backroom tactics, the presidency went to Jefferson and the vice-presidency to Burr. Burr, insulted by Hamilton's behavior, ultimately challenged him to a duel and killed him. The nation was then confronted with the spectacle of witnessing a murder charge filed against one of the country's leading officials for the death of another Founding Father.

20

The end result of the tricks by Hamilton and his allies was the passage of the Twelfth Amendment to the Constitution, which sought to clear up the voting procedure in the electoral college. The amendment provided for the members "to name in their ballots the person voted for as President and in distinct ballots the person voted for as Vice President." Thus in 1804 the electors began casting separate votes—an important step toward ensuring that the will of the people would be honored in national elections.

By 1824, when John Quincy Adams (son of John Adams) was elected president, the nation had begun choosing presidential electors by popular, rather than legislative, vote. John Quincy Adams's chief opponent was Andrew Jackson, who led a crowded field of contenders in the popular vote by about 50,000 ballots. But since Jackson did not have a majority of the electoral votes, the contest was thrown into the House of Representatives.

There, backroom deals resulted in Adams's election. His opponents accused Adams of winning the presidency through a "corrupt bargain." After all, they noted, Jackson had received 99 votes in the electoral college to Adams's 84. Although Jackson's total fell short of a majority, it seemed to indicate the will of the people; only the supposedly "corrupt bargain" in the House vote had put Adams in the White House, his critics charged. Although the allegation was neither proved nor disproved, it left a bitter aftertaste. Four years later, when Adams sought re-election, he lost by a wide margin to Jackson.

Though many elections have been tainted by charges

21

of fraud, experts generally agree that the most flagrant theft of a national election occurred in 1876. The major candidates were Democrat Samuel J. Tilden and Republican Rutherford B. Hayes. Large numbers of votes were stolen by each side.

In the South, the locations of many polling places were switched on election day in attempts to confuse black voters, who were expected to favor Hayes. Ku Klux Klansmen armed with rifles appeared at other polling places and turned away black voters. In some cases, when blacks were escorted to the polling places by United States marshals, both they and the marshals were shot by Klansmen.

On the Republican side, President Ulysses S. Grant used every possible means—including military force—to try to ensure Hayes's election. Two days after the election, Tilden led Hayes in the popular vote by about 250,000; he also led in the electoral vote by 184 to 166. But 185 electoral votes were required for election, and the electoral votes of three southern states—South Carolina, Florida, and Louisiana—were still in doubt.

Although Tilden had apparently carried all three states, the results had been contested by the Republicans controlling these Reconstruction state governments. If the results could be swung to Hayes in the three states, he was assured of the presidency by an electoral majority of 1 vote.

In each state, there were two factions with separate electoral boards contesting for the right to certify the results. One faction consisted of the Republican carpetbaggers who had come from the North and the blacks who followed their lead; the other consisted of local whites, virtually all of them Democrats. Each board claimed it was "official" and had sole right to tabulate the results.

President Grant sent federal troops into the three states to enforce the carpetbaggers' vote tallies at bayonet point. With the military support, the Republicans resorted to every imaginable device to steal the election from Tilden. In Louisiana, the Republican electoral board simply tossed out 13,000 Tilden votes. In Florida, where Tilden held a decisive majority, the Republican board ignored the results and declared Hayes the winner.

Ultimately, Congress passed a law creating a special commission to decide the election. The commission—composed of five members of the Senate, five members of the House, and five Supreme Court justices—included seven Democrats, seven Republicans, and one justice who was supposed to be neutral.

The commission split along straight party lines, with the seven Democrats all ruling in favor of Tilden and the seven Republicans in favor of Hayes. Thus the decision was left to the supposedly neutral justice, Joseph B. Bradley. Early in the life of the commission, Bradley had written a preliminary opinion supporting Tilden's election. But after spending the entire night before the final decision in the company of a Republican cabinet member and a Republican senator, he voted to give the election to Hayes. It was the only time in American history that a president had been "elected" with fewer popular votes than his opponent. Of course, there is justifiable cause to believe that

23

Hayes was never elected at all—that he reached the White House only through the most cynical sort of fraud.

In recent years, the most celebrated cases of purported election fraud occurred during John F. Kennedy's campaign for the presidency. In the early primaries, Senator Hubert H. Humphrey was Kennedy's chief opponent. Although he was popular among voters and party officials, Humphrey was handicapped by a severe shortage of campaign funds. Kennedy seemingly had more than enough campaign money and was constantly accused of intending to "buy" the election with his father's millions. In response, Kennedy often joked that he had just received a telegram from home. He said the telegram, written by his father, read: "Dear Jack—Don't buy a single vote more than is necessary. I'll be damned if I'm going to pay for a landslide."

Joke or not, serious allegations of vote buying were leveled against the Kennedy campaign organization. The first such charges of consequence came in the West Virginia primary. Even before voters went to the polls, Senator Humphrey charged that entire election districts had been bought by the Kennedy forces.

It was nothing new for political organizations to pay West Virginians a few dollars each to show up at the polls on election day. Theoretically, at least, the money was to reimburse voters for transportation costs in reaching the polling places. And, also theoretically, they then had the right to cast their ballots any way they chose. But in practice West Virginians who accepted such money usually voted the way they were told. In the primary, the voters gave Kennedy a significant victory and knocked Humphrey out of the race for the Democratic nomination. All available evidence indicates some of them were paid to vote for Kennedy. But no clear proof has ever been produced to indicate that Kennedy or his key aides were directly involved in the vote-buying effort. In any event, Kennedy probably would have won the primary without such illegal help. The West Virginia primary, along with those in several other important states, put him clearly on the road to the Democratic nomination. He was nominated for president on the first ballot at the Democratic national convention and chose Lyndon Johnson as his vice-presidential candidate.

At the Republican convention, Vice President Richard M. Nixon was selected as the presidential candidate. He picked as his running mate the man Kennedy had defeated in his initial Massachusetts Senate race, Henry Cabot Lodge, member of a noted New England family.

It was a bitterly fought campaign, and by election day it was clear that the race would be extremely close. Texas and Illinois, with long histories of election fraud, were particularly critical to the outcome. George Parr, who had helped steal the 1948 Senate election for Lyndon Johnson, still dominated the political life of a wide area of southern Texas. In the 1960 election, he delivered the usual lopsided majority for his old comrade, Johnson, and the entire Democratic ticket. But Parr was not the only wheeler-dealer in Texas to be accused of election fraud in the 1960 race. Nixon would eventually charge that votes had been stolen throughout the state, helping to put the important bloc of Texas electoral votes in the Kennedy-Johnson column.

Even more blatant were the theft and purchase of votes in Illinois. Investigations by newspapers and Republican officials resulted in allegations that the powerful Democratic machine headed by Chicago Mayor Richard Daley—one of Kennedy's staunchest allies—had been responsible for widespread ballot irregularities. In some cases, skid row derelicts, many of them drunk and unable to comprehend the ballots, were run through polling places by old-line Illinois Democratic politicians. The derelicts voted under the names of persons who had died years earlier but had never been removed from the registration lists.

In other cases, the Democratic organization made use of election cheats known as "short-pencil artists." The "artists" were Democratic election officials assigned to count the votes, particularly in Chicago and surrounding Cook County. They held short pencils in their hands or stuck pencil leads under their fingernails while counting the votes. When they came across votes cast for Nixon, the cheats used the hidden pencils or leads to deface some of the ballots. After being defaced, the ballots were disqualified and thus did not count in Nixon's column.

The Kennedy-Johnson ticket carried Illinois by only 8,000 votes, and Nixon claimed he had been cheated out of far more votes than that. The Democrats, while admitting to no fraud themselves, accused the Republicans of smearing their reputations and claimed the Republicans had done their own vote stealing. In the end, Illinois prosecutors ordered the arrest of no fewer than 667 Democratic election officials on a variety of charges. But most of the charges were dismissed amid a tangle of claims and counterclaims.

In his memoirs, *Six Crises*, Nixon contended that votes stolen from him in Texas and Illinois had cost him the 1960 election. But he chose not to contest the outcome in the courts, which he could have done. Nixon claimed he refrained from doing so because the election-challenge process was so complicated in Texas and Illinois that the issue would have dragged on for months, perhaps years.

As Nixon put it: "From the evidence I examined, there was no question but that there was real substance to many of these charges. . . . But substance or not, when I looked into the legal aspects of the situation, I found that it would take at least a year and a half to get a recount in Illinois and that there was no procedure whatever for a losing candidate to get a recount in Texas."

Although Nixon may have overstated the case, it is unquestionably true that efforts to recount fraudulent election results are fraught with difficulties. In many cases, the very politicians who have stolen the election control the machinery (if it exists) for reviewing ballot results. Sometimes an absence of legislation in a particular state makes it almost impossible to reverse initial election tallies. Although there is always the possibility of a lawsuit, history has shown that courts are usually reluctant to involve themselves in the election process.

3 HOW ELECTIONS ARE STOLEN

Illinois, Texas, and West Virginia are just three areas among many that have been susceptible to election fraud. Through the years, powerful political machines, determined to preserve their influence no matter what the cost, have stolen election after election in such areas with shocking regularity. Bribes have been paid to voters for casting their ballots in favor of machine candidates. Election officials have looked the other way while individuals have voted three, four, or even more times. Voting machines have been rigged. And certain law enforcement officers have allowed it all to happen, often because they have owed their jobs to the corrupt political machines involved.

The disputed 1960 Kennedy election results in

Illinois—particularly Chicago and surrounding Cook County—were part of a long history of dirty politics in that area. Unfortunately, it is a history to which fresh chapters continue to be added with almost every succeeding election. Just two years later, a Chicago newspaper published photographs of local Democratic officials paying derelicts to vote in a Senate election. Reporters interviewed the voters, who said they had been steered from the polling places to a nearby building loft and had illegally been provided bottles of cheap wine.

In 1969 two Chicago election officials and a local policewoman were arrested on charges involving similar election irregularities. They were accused of paying skid row derelicts to register to vote.

The FBI has jurisdiction over fraud cases in federal elections. In 1972, when still another election scandal erupted in Chicago, FBI agents were called in to investigate. They arrested forty election officials, Democrats and Republicans alike, on charges of carrying out voting frauds during primary elections. Among those arrested were eighteen Republican election judges, sixteen Democratic judges, three Democratic precinct captains, and three Democratic assistant captains.

United States Attorney James Thompson, Jr., said a lengthy investigation by his office and a grand jury uncovered "vote fraud on a massive, pervasive scale." The defendants were charged with forging ballot applications, signing fraudulent ballot applications, allowing unsigned ballot applications to be counted, and permitting persons to vote in precincts in which they were not legal residents. Thompson said further:

29

My only interest is in insuring that votes honestly cast in federal elections are honestly counted. To the extent that votes are fraudulently cast or unlawfully counted, the votes of each of us as citizens are diminished. Democrats, Republicans or independents, we are all a little poorer as citizens and democracy is degraded when election officials do not fulfill their responsibilities to protect and count our votes.

Like Chicago, Kansas City, Missouri, is an area that has been plagued by frequent ballot box frauds. From the 1930s to the 1950s, the Kansas City political machine assembled by Democratic boss Tom Pendergast was involved in an almost constant series of election scandals. The FBI was first called in to investigate irregularities in Kansas City after the 1936 elections.

Agents built up damning evidence of fraud, stuffing of ballot boxes, intimidation of voters, and theft of votes through the changing of ballot markings from Republican to Democratic candidates. In the resulting trials, 256 defendants—many of them the very election officials who were assigned to keep the balloting honest—were convicted of fraud.

But the Pendergast machine was persistent. In 1946 the FBI was called in again—this time to investigate a Democratic primary race for a congressional seat. Enos Axtell, the candidate supported by President Harry S Truman (himself a product of the Pendergast machine) defeated incumbent Roger Slaughter in the primary. Slaughter claimed fraud, and the FBI was supposed to examine the ballots. Then, one midnight before the examination could be conducted, burglars blew up the election-board vault containing the ballots. The FBI investigation resulted in sending a syndicate racketeer—in the hire of the Pendergast machine—to prison for the dynamiting. But the election results were allowed to stand because the evidence of election fraud had been destroyed in the explosion.

Later, still other election scandals erupted and a congressional investigation was ordered. It stretched into the 1950s and ended with a congressional committee issuing a sharp denunciation of Supreme Court Justice Tom Clark for his purported whitewashing of the Kansas City frauds while serving as President Truman's attorney general. The committee charged that Clark had tied the hands of FBI agents assigned to investigate the scandals by ordering the agents to limit their investigation to interviewing six specified witnesses. Thus the agents had been prevented from pursuing leads that might well have led to prosecution of prominent political figures, the committee reported.

New York City has also witnessed more than its share of election scandals. Tammany Hall, the powerful political organization that dominated New York City politics for generations, was responsible for many of them.

In the early 1900s Tammany's control of some New York neighborhoods was so influential that many families knew they would be deprived of their livelihoods if they opposed the political machine. Jobs were handed out wholesale by local political bosses on the basis of loyalty to the Democratic organization. Wage earners knew they faced the prospect of getting fired

31

and not being able to find other work if they were caught supporting Republican candidates.

Still, there were some who risked their financial stability by secretly voting against Tammany's tyrannical rule. In an attempt to enforce party loyalty at the polls, Tammany then resorted to an unusual form of harassment. In those days, the candidates of all parties did not appear on a single ballot. Therefore, when a voter reached the polling place, he would ask for a Democratic ballot, a Republican ballot, or a ballot for one of the minor parties. He would then mark the ballot and drop it in the box. When Tammany officials became suspicious that some of their supposed followers were defecting to the opposition, they impregnated all the Democratic ballots with a chemical that had a powerful, long-lasting odor. Then, when the voters emerged from the polling places, their hands were subjected to "sniff" tests by an official Tammany smeller. Those who flunked could expect to lose their jobs and suffer other reprisals.

In later years, Tammany mastered the technique of using "repeater" voters—that is, voters who cast several ballots in the same election. Men with beards were favorite repeaters, for their appearance could easily be changed. For example, a man would vote the first time with a full beard. He would then be taken by a Tammany political hack to a barber, who would shave off the man's chin whiskers—but not his mustache or sideburns. The repeater would vote a second time, then return to have his sideburns removed but his mustache left intact. After voting a third time, he would go to the barber to have his mustache shaved, then he would cast a fourth ballot clean-shaven. Since Tammany controlled the election records, its opponents were unable to prevent the fraud.

Repeater voting is still practiced in New York and is not confined to Democrats. After one recent Republican primary, police arrested a Manhattan man who admitted voting sixty-eight times.

But the most consistent and sophisticated election frauds in New York were carried out by Tammany Hall. One favorite Tammany trick was to set up a dummy polling place in a Republican-controlled district. The dummy looked exactly like an official voting place equipped with voting booths, poll watchers, and all the trappings. Tammany workers would then go to an official polling place that had long lines of citizens waiting to vote. They would tell the voters there was another poll nearby, where ballots could be cast without waiting. The voters would then be led to the dummy polling place, enter the booths, and "vote." Of course, those votes would never be tallied. And since it was a Republican-controlled district, the lost votes were bound to work to the Democrats' advantage.

Occasionally, allegations of fraud have prompted the New York courts to step in and reverse the announced election results. In 1966, for example, the State Supreme Court ruled that there had been widespread fraud in a Manhattan congressional primary between incumbent Representative Leonard Farbstein and his challenger, City Councilman Theodore Weiss. Farbstein had apparently won the primary by 151 votes, but Weiss challenged the results in a lawsuit and the court found that at least 1,153 fraudulent votes had been cast. The court invalidated Farbstein's victory and ordered a new primary. Farbstein won again and Weiss charged that the second primary had also been marred by fraud, but the result was allowed to stand. That same year, four primaries in the Bronx were also invalidated by the courts because of fraud. In another incident several years later, an official of the New York City Board of Elections was arrested by FBI agents on charges of conspiring to insert into the voter-registration records names of persons who were not legally registered.

Some of New York State's most flagrant election frauds, however, have occurred not in New York City but in the state capital of Albany. One such case occurred in 1954 during the election in which Democrat W. Averell Harriman was elected governor by a narrow margin. An investigation disclosed that the Albany Democratic organization had bought the votes of more than 16,000 citizens, at five dollars a head. Moreover, absentee ballots had been stolen and forged; people too young to be eligible as voters had been allowed to cast ballots; and unregistered derelicts had been herded from flop houses to the polls. Despite the overwhelming evidence of fraud, Harriman's victory was permitted to stand.

Similar frauds have been exposed regularly in succeeding years in Albany. In 1967 a grand jury conducted a major investigation into vote buying and other frauds. The investigation was launched after a group of citizens, led by prominent clergymen, charged that voters in Albany's slum areas had again been paid five dollars each to "vote the right way."

Some ghetto residents openly admitted that their votes had been bought. One typical resident, Leon Van Dyke, told news reporters: "Why did I take the five dollars? Because I was broke, and five dollars is a lot of money to me. It's a practice people down here take for granted. The only reason people here come out to vote is because they're going to get the five dollars. If the practice stopped, voting would drop considerably."

The results of the grand jury investigation, however, were inconsequential, and the irregularities were allowed to continue unabated.

New York State Republicans have also been involved in their share of election scandals. One such case involved a group of Long Island Republican officials who were charged with padding their registration rolls with the names of at least 1,000 phantom voters.

Sometimes allegations of ballot irregularities crop up in areas that have not had long histories of election fraud. Such was the case in 1952 in New Mexico. Senator Dennis Chavez was opposed for re-election by Patrick S. Hurley, a former U.S. ambassador to China. Chavez claimed victory by a margin of about 5,000 votes, but Hurley protested that there had been numerous election law violations. An investigation by New Mexico authorities turned up wholesale evidence of such violations, including widespread destruction of ballots, voting by aliens, and systematic denial of the right to vote in secret. Since the Senate has a constitutional right to determine the legal qualifications of its members, a Senate committee conducted a lengthy investigation of its own. The committee reported find-

35

ing so many irregularities that it was impossible to determine who had won the election. By a vote of 5 to 4, it recommended that the Senate declare the election void and oust Chavez from office pending a new election. But the full Senate voted 53 to 36 against taking such action and permitted Chavez to retain his seat.

The Senate action touched off widespread criticism. It was charged that the Senate—long known as the nation's most exclusive "club"—had ignored extensive evidence of fraud because it was determined to avoid ousting one of its members. Despite the criticism, however, Chavez retained his Senate seat and privileges.

An even more complex case was presented to the Senate following a disputed election for a New Hampshire senatorial seat in 1974. The first tally of votes appeared to give the Republican candidate, Congressman Louis C. Wyman, a victory by only 355 votes out of more than 220,000 that had been cast. But Wyman's Democratic opponent, former State Insurance Commissioner John A. Durkin, demanded a recount by New Hampshire's Republican secretary of state, Robert L. Stark. After conducting the recount, Stark ruled that Durkin had won the election by 10 votes. Then, however, Wyman asked for still another recount—this one by the New Hampshire Ballot Law Commission, all of whose members had been appointed by Republican governors. The commission reviewed about 400 disputed ballots and decided that Wyman had won by 2 votes.

Durkin then appealed to the Senate, and it struggled with the issue for seven months, considering claims of ballot irregularities from both sides. Finally, on July

30, 1975, the Senate declared its "inability" to settle the dispute. It declared the New Hampshire Senate seat vacant, setting the stage for a new election. That contest, a rematch between Durkin and Wyman, took place on September 16, 1975, and resulted in a decisive victory for Democrat Durkin, who got 140,273 votes to Wyman's 113,003.

For those bent on stealing elections, the possibilities seem almost endless. Some of their favorite tricks revolve around the rigging of voting machines. George Abrams, chief investigator for a citizens' election-monitoring group known as the Honest Ballot Association, says: "Voting machines run by honest people can be fraud-proof. But any machine in the hands of crooks is not."

It is possible, for example, to manipulate one small mechanical part of a voting machine in advance so as to stop a candidate's total vote tally at a predetermined figure. Often, crooked precinct workers cast large numbers of votes for their candidates before the polls even open. They then cover the voting machines' tabulation meters with pieces of paper reading "000"—indicating that no votes have been registered. Election judges, seeing the zeros, lock the machines for the beginning of the voting. As the balloting proceeds and the cylinders on the machines turn, the paper bearing the zeros rolls off, displaying the fraudulent vote totals.

Another technique used by unscrupulous election officials is to jam the levers beside an opposition candidate's name on the voting machines. When voters try to push down the levers to vote for such a candidate,

37

they find that the levers will not move. Often, in frustration, they simply give up. In one recent election in San Antonio, Texas, voters found that virtually all the levers for one political party had been jammed. In another election, in Jefferson County, Kentucky, the local election board received more than 150 calls reporting jammed machines during the first hour of voting. Many citizens waited up to an hour for repairmen to arrive, then left the polls in disgust without voting.

Sometimes, crooked election officials cover a candidate's name on the voting machine with tape or deliberately place the name in the wrong column to deceive voters. As investigator George Abrams put it: "Often, a half day's voting passes with a candidate's name in a wrong column. His voters unknowingly cast ballots for someone else."

Election workers also cheat at times by giving voters incorrect instructions on how to use the machines. After two consecutive Pennsylvania elections, lawsuits produced evidence that thousands of votes had been registered for blank spaces on machines because citizens had been given improper instructions. A New Jersey election aroused suspicion over an abnormally large number of votes cast for a minority party whose ballot tally normally was minuscule. Investigation revealed that many voters mistakenly cast their ballots for the minority party after being told to push levers beneath, rather than above, the name of the major party for which they really wanted to vote.

Many citizens who receive welfare payments or hold jobs dispensed by political organizations not only vote the way they are told, but agree to participate in ballot fraud. Some, too unsophisticated or with inadequate memories to follow the political organizations' instructions on how to vote, pretend to be blind—so that party workers will be allowed to accompany them into the polling booths and operate the machines for them. Others claim to have crippling diseases that prevent them from operating the machines. Still others pretend they are afraid of the machines. The party workers who help them vote, of course, push the levers favoring the party of their own choice.

When one party dominates a community's election board, it may try to hold down the opposition party's vote by sending insufficient numbers of voting machines to polling places in areas with heavy concentrations of opposition constituents. Just one machine may be sent to a precinct that requires several. As a result, long lines develop at the polls. Voters become impatient, and many of them leave the polling places without casting their ballots.

Another means of cheating involves simply reporting inaccurately the ballot totals that appear on the voting machines. Often, poll workers deliberately transpose the figures that appear on the machines. If an opposing candidate receives 291 votes, for example, the poll workers may report the total as 192. In flagrant cases, cheaters may go as far as to delete one or more digits from the reported vote tally. After one Chicago election, an investigation revealed that at least thirty-two machine totals had been inaccurately reported. One candidate received 207 votes on a certain machine, but only 7 votes were reported. Another received 44 votes, but only 4 were recorded.

39

Obviously, the most practical means of preventing such frauds is to have trained representatives of all parties present at every polling place to keep watch on each other. But in areas where one party dominates the political scene, it is sometimes difficult for minority parties to find volunteers to man the polls. In the absence of watchful eyes from their opponents, the controlling party's representatives are able to steal any votes necessary to ensure continued dominance.

4 LEGALIZED ELECTION THIEVERY

Not all "thefts" of votes are crimes. Built into the American political system over the years have been numerous means of unfairly influencing the outcome of elections without breaking the law.

For years, citizens in many areas of the United States were deprived of the right to have their votes carry equal weight with those of fellow residents of their states. Their disadvantage resulted from a discriminatory system of apportioning seats in the state legislatures and, in some cases, in the U.S. House of Representatives—a system that gave far greater weight to votes cast in thinly populated rural areas than to those cast in heavily populated cities and suburbs.

The situation prevailing in Tennessee by the late 1950s was typical of those in many areas throughout

41

the country. Apportionment of seats in the Tennessee legislature was still based on a system adopted almost sixty years earlier. During those six decades, vast changes had occurred in the population patterns of Tennessee. Because of industrial growth and other factors, many residents had left rural areas and moved to the cities and rapidly burgeoning suburbs. But the apportionment of seats in the legislature had not been revised to account for these population shifts.

Thus, for example, rural Moore County and urban Hamilton County each had the identical number of seats in the legislature. But the population of Hamilton County was nineteen times that of Moore County. So, in effect, the vote of a resident of Hamilton County carried only one-nineteenth the weight of that cast by a Moore County resident.

Parallel circumstances prevailed throughout the state. As a result, a mere 37 percent of Tennessee's voters were responsible for electing twenty of the thirty-three senators and 40 percent of the voters were responsible for electing sixty-three of the ninety-nine representatives in their state legislature.

Since most of the legislators had been elected by rural voters, they catered to rural interests in drafting bills. The resulting rural domination of the legislation brought about a system in which the critical needs of Tennessee's cities were often neglected.

Urban voters made numerous attempts to remedy the unfair apportionment system. They sought changes in both the apportionment law and the state constitution. But since such changes required the approval of both houses of the legislature, they invariably failed.

The rural lawmakers—unwilling to surrender any of their power—defeated all measures aimed at establishing legislative districts tied more closely to equal population patterns.

Finally, a group of urban Tennessee residents, headed by a man named Charles W. Baker, filed a federal court suit seeking to overturn the state apportionment law. The suit, contending that the law was unconstitutional, asked for a court order barring the state from conducting any more elections until the statute was changed. On the surface, at least, Baker's suit seemed to stand little chance of success. The federal courts had historically taken a hands-off attitude toward legislative apportionment disputes. In one notable decision, Supreme Court Justice Felix Frankfurter had written that reapportionment was a "political thicket" the courts should not enter.

Thus it was hardly surprising that Baker and his colleagues lost the first round in their suit. A federal district court dismissed the case, claiming that it lacked jurisdiction and that the suit had not sought remedies the court could practically grant.

But Baker and his colleagues persevered, appealing the decision all the way to the Supreme Court. On March 26, 1962, the Supreme Court reversed the lower court ruling dismissing the case. By a 6-to-3 vote, the Court ruled that Baker and his fellow complainants— as voters and taxpayers—had the right to file suit testing the constitutionality of the state apportionment law. The Supreme Court said federal courts had the power to resolve the matter by ordering reapportionment of the legislature if the facts warranted such action. It sent the case back to the federal district court for a full hearing on the issues to determine whether the Tennessee apportionment system did, indeed, discriminate against urban voters.

The Supreme Court ruling in the Baker suit represented a milestone, for it asserted for the first time that the federal courts had jurisdiction over apportionment cases. It thus touched off a flood of lawsuits similar to the Baker case, filed by voters in all sections of the country. In case after case, the federal courts were asked to overturn apportionment systems that discriminated against urban and suburban voters. The cases presented complex issues, and the most significant of them ultimately were carried to the Supreme Court.

On June 15, 1964, the Supreme Court handed down a landmark decision that was to set the pattern for numerous other rulings in apportionment cases. The ruling established a standard of "one man, one vote" in apportioning legislative seats. That is, legislative districts were to be drawn up as nearly as possible on the basis of equal population.

The decision came in a case in which the Court overturned the apportionment of the Alabama legislature, which urban voters contended discriminated against them. One rural Alabama state Senate district contained only 31,175 residents, while an urban district in Birmingham contained 634,864. Population of districts in the state House of Representatives ranged from a rural low of 10,726 to an urban high of 42,303. The Supreme Court ruled, by a 6-3 margin, that such disparities made the Alabama apportionment system unconstitutional. Both houses of the Alabama legislature would have to be reapportioned on the basis of population under the "one man, one vote" doctrine. That same day, the Court employed the doctrine in deciding apportionment cases from five other states—Maryland, Delaware, Colorado, New York, and Virginia.

In the months and years that followed, the "one man, one vote" rule was used by the federal courts in ordering reapportionment of numerous other legislatures. Such revisions represented major steps in eliminating the discrimination that had long plagued urban and suburban voters.

Another means of using the apportionment process to bring about unfair voting results is known as a gerrymander—a technique for drawing election-district lines in a manner designed to favor one party or candidate. The word gerrymander is derived from the name of Elbridge Gerry, who served as governor of Massachusetts in the early 1800s and then as vice president of the United States during James Madison's second administration. In 1812, while Gerry was governor, the Massachusetts legislature—controlled by Gerry's allies in what was then known as the Democratic-Republican party—passed a bill that divided the state into districts for the election of state senators. The district lines were drawn in such a way that certain counties in which the rival Federalist party held large majorities were lumped together in irregular fashion. As a result, the Federalists would be able to win only a few legislative seats—all by lopsided majorities. But the Democratic-Republicans, with their supporters distributed on a relatively even basis throughout the remaining districts, would be able to win many more seats by slender majorities.

45

Despite Federalist complaints that the districting bill unfairly discriminated against them, Governor Gerry signed the measure into law. One of the newly created districts had a weird shape that some said looked like a prehistoric creature. Others said it looked like a salamander. During a discussion of the subject at a dinner party, one guest suggested that—in view of Gerry's signing of the new law—the district should be called a "gerrymander." The name stuck, and has become part of the American language as a term describing discriminatory districting procedures. Gerrymandering has persisted throughout the years and is still practiced today.

State legislatures have the power to draw the lines for elections both for their own members' districts and for congressional districts. The party controlling a legislature is able to dictate the manner in which the district lines are drafted. Experts on political map-making, employed by the legislative majority, study past election records to determine the party allegiances of groups of voters in various geographic areas throughout the state. In carrying out a gerrymandering plan, they then draw the district lines in a way that will give their party the maximum political advantage.

A study of congressional elections in several states in 1962, conducted by Professor Andrew Hacker of the Cornell University Department of Government, presented a vivid picture of how gerrymandering influences the outcome of elections. The study showed, for example, that California Democrats—who controlled the legislature and thus were empowered to draw the congressional district lines—managed to win 66 percent of the state's thirty-eight congressional seats, although their supporters cast only 52 percent of the votes. In Michigan, the results of gerrymandering were even more striking. The Republicans in control of the legislature there succeeded in winning 61 percent of the state's eighteen congressional seats even though their voters constituted a minority (48 percent) of the electorate.

By and large, except for enforcing the "one man, one vote" rule, the courts are reluctant to interfere in apportionment disputes. Judges generally feel the issues involved should be decided by the political, rather than the judicial, process. Thus there is every reason to believe that gerrymanders will continue to be part of the American political system.

Unfair apportionment practices have represented only one of several forms of voting discrimination practiced against various groups of Americans. Among those who were deprived of the vote for many years were American women. Nowadays, when women outnumber men in the United States and theoretically could elect a female president if they voted as a bloc, it is sometimes forgotten that participation in elections was an exclusively male preserve until 1920. The woman's suffrage movement, long a subject of derision, accomplished its purpose through protest marches, rallies, speeches, and organized pressure by wives against their own husbands.

Today, while women have the vote, they are often discriminated against in other ways when they seek active roles in politics. Traditionally, when women have enlisted as volunteers in political campaigns, they have been given the work involving the most drudgery—stuffing and licking envelopes, and making telephone

47

calls to citizens—while their male counterparts have been given policy-making roles. Most political leaders concede that their most loyal, effective grass-roots workers are often women. Yet, when the time comes to choose candidates, political parties turn to women only rarely.

Some observers have noted that cases in which women have been guilty of practicing dirty politics have been rare. Such a generalization, of course, may be misleading. It may simply be that women have not had sufficient opportunity to practice dirty politics because they have been denied top roles in most campaigns. But advocates of greater participation by women in politics say they deserve the chance to try doing better than men have in the past.

Another form of discrimination—based on racial and ethnic heritage—prevented many Americans from exercising their right to vote for almost a century. After the end of the Reconstruction that followed the Civil War, virtually all blacks were excluded from voting in the South.

Whites who controlled the political power structures in southern states used every possible technique to prevent blacks from registering and voting. In some cases, blacks who tried to register were threatened, assaulted, and even killed. Poll taxes—special taxes that were to be paid as a requirement for voting—were imposed in efforts to discourage poor blacks from trying to register. Extremely difficult written tests, containing highly technical questions about obscure sections of the U.S. Constitution and various laws, were given to blacks as requirements for proving they were "qualified" to vote.

In some areas, blacks who tried to register were told they must produce previously registered voters to vouch for their integrity and good character. Since those already registered invariably were whites who opposed voting by blacks, the chances of obtaining such character witnesses were minuscule. Consequently, only small numbers of blacks managed to register and vote in the South, and their effect on the electoral process was negligible.

Such methods were used in spite of clear constitutional prohibitions against denying Americans the right to vote on racial grounds. The Fifteenth Amendment to the Constitution provides, among other things, that "the right of citizens of the United States to vote shall not be denied or abridged by the United States or by any state on account of race, color or previous condition of servitude." And the Fourteenth Amendment provides that "no state shall make or enforce any law which shall abridge the privileges and immunities of citizens of the United States . . . nor deny to any person within its jurisdiction the equal protection of the laws."

During the civil rights movement of the 1950s and 1960s, as gains were made in such fields as desegregation of schools and other public facilities, widespread efforts were launched to end racial discrimination in voting. Many of these efforts were met with violent resistance. Three civil rights workers were waylaid and murdered in Mississippi. A clergyman was clubbed to death by four segregationists while taking part in a protest demonstration in Selma, Alabama. A woman was shot to death after participating in a protest march from Selma to Montgomery. Club-swinging members of

49

a sheriff's posse inflicted heavy casualties on other demonstrators in several confrontations in Selma.

Against that background, President Lyndon B. Johnson proposed and pushed through Congress a historic law aimed at eliminating racial discrimination in voting. The measure, known as the Voting Rights Act of 1965, contained a wide range of remedies for such discrimination. A series of amendments to the law passed in 1970 broadened the act's scope still further.

The law prohibits the use of literacy tests or similar exams as requirements for voting in federal, state, and local elections. It also rules out payment of a poll tax as a condition for voting. In counties and states where continued attempts to discriminate against voting applicants take place, the U.S. attorney general is empowered to assign federal examiners to register voters on a nondiscriminatory basis. The attorney general is also authorized to send federal observers to such areas to ensure that all eligible citizens are allowed to vote and that ballots are accurately counted.

The law provides criminal penalties for public officials or private individuals who deny an individual the right to vote guaranteed by the statute. Anyone who tries to intimidate, threaten, or coerce a person in order to prevent him from voting is also subject to criminal penalties. The law makes it a crime, as well, to try to intimidate, threaten, or coerce anyone who urges or aids any person to vote. In addition, it authorizes the attorney general to file lawsuits to restrain violations of the Voting Rights Act.

Following passage of the law, great strides were made in curbing racial discrimination in voting. Strict enforcement of the law discouraged white officials from continuing to interfere with blacks' efforts to register and vote. By mid-1976, more than 3½ million blacks had registered in the South. In many areas, blacks had been elected to public office for the first time.

Blacks were not the only members of minority groups to benefit from the new law. In the Southwest, for example, the statute was used to win voting rights long denied to many Mexican-Americans. In New York and other urban areas, the law helped bring about increased registration of immigrants from Puerto Rico and elsewhere in Latin America. As a follow-up to passage of the law, some areas with large concentrations of Spanish-speaking citizens began printing their ballots in both English and Spanish to facilitate voting.

Still, every election day brings complaints from one section or another that minority-group members continue to suffer discrimination. The U.S. Department of Justice has vigorously pressed state and local authorities to eliminate such discrimination. It continues sending federal observers into specified counties, particularly in the South, where blacks and members of other minorities have been victims of discrimination. State and local officials—most notably, Alabama's George Wallace—have argued that these so-called "invasions" by federal observers amount to imposition of dictatorial control from Washington. Although there is a danger of the federal government becoming so active in trying to protect minority rights that it tramples on majority rights, the long history of voting discrimination in some areas indicates a need for continued vigilance.

51

PART TWO

SPYING, SABOTAGE, AND SMEAR CAMPAIGNS

5 CLOUDS OVER THE KENNEDY CAMPAIGN

Until John F. Kennedy's election in 1960, no Catholic had ever occupied the White House. The Democrats had nominated a Catholic, New York Governor Alfred E. (Al) Smith, against Herbert Hoover in 1928, only to see him soundly defeated. For years afterward, some political observers said that no Catholic would ever again be nominated for president by a major party, much less elected.

When it became clear that Kennedy was a serious contender for the Democratic nomination, the issue of his Catholicism was exploited not only by politicians but also by self-appointed vigilantes bent on ensuring that the White House would remain the private preserve of white Protestants. Fundamentalist religious sects,

55

among others, began circulating "smear" literature claiming the pope would dominate the United States if a Catholic were to win the presidency. Some of these smear sheets went as far as to claim that Kennedy had already promised to build a secret tunnel under the Atlantic to Europe so that the pope could travel to Washington incognito and give orders to the new Catholic president. This notion, on its face absurd, was believed by some naive Americans.

Many equally absurd lies about Catholic beliefs and practices were circulated, all in attempts to undermine Kennedy's candidacy. On Long Island, for example, a Baptist minister circulated a leaflet among his parishioners contending that a pope had once threatened to hang all his enemies. The leaflet was a fraud. Yet identical copies soon turned up in Pennsylvania, California, and many Bible Belt states in the South and Midwest.

Not all the criticism of Kennedy's candidacy on religious grounds came from charlatans. Several groups of reputable Protestant clergymen announced from their pulpits that they would oppose Kennedy's candidacy unless he assured the public of his independence from papal influence.

It should be noted that none of Kennedy's opponents publicly raised the religious issue in an attempt to head off his drive for the presidential nomination. But the increasing attention given the issue in the news media invariably led politicians to spend disproportionate lengths of time discussing Kennedy's religion—rather than his record and his position on various policies. Thus, throughout the primary campaigns, Kennedy was on the defensive. He was forced to prove that a wealthy

Catholic from a family of Boston Irish politicians could win national support.

Senator Kennedy confronted the religious issue squarely in his West Virginia primary campaign. The state was predominantly Protestant, and Kennedy encountered many voters who saw little difference on issues among the major presidential candidates but did not "want a Catholic for president."

In response, Kennedy insisted in a series of campaign appearances: "I refuse to believe that I was denied the right to be President on the day I was baptized." Finally, he went on television and addressed the issue of religious intolerance:

> When any man stands on the steps of the Capitol and takes the oath of office of President, he is swearing to support the separation of church and state. He puts one hand on the Bible and raises the other hand to God as he takes the oath. And, if he breaks the oath, he is not only committing a crime against the Constitution, for which Congress can impeach him—and should impeach him—but he is committing a sin against God.

Despite the charges of voting fraud in the West Virginia primary, Kennedy's victory accomplished its chief purpose—it blunted the religious issue. Once Kennedy had shown he could win in a heavily Protestant state, his opponents could no longer argue that his religion would prevent him from defeating the Republican nominee in the November election.

Thus another sort of smear campaign was mounted

against Kennedy as he continued his quest for the nomination. Stories began surfacing in the news media—usually attributed to unidentified sources—that Kennedy was seriously ill.

In some respects, these tales were harder for Kennedy to counter than the religious attacks. He could, at least, confront that issue directly. But the anonymous yarns about his health were so wispy that Kennedy could not adequately rebut them without giving them additional credibility. They stemmed from problems traceable to his service in World War II as a navy officer.

Kennedy was said to suffer from an insufficiency of adrenalin and was known to have spent several long sieges in hospitals because of a nagging back injury. Nonetheless, he seemed at other times the picture of good health and took pains to project the image of a youthful, vibrant man. He was photographed sailing, playing golf, participating in family touch football games, and otherwise displaying his athletic prowess. But the pictures did not show the brace he wore most of the time to ease his back pain.

When it appeared likely Kennedy would win the Democratic presidential nomination unless some roadblock appeared in his way, forces supporting Lyndon Johnson for president resorted to a whispering campaign that vastly overstated Kennedy's health problems. It was said he was suffering from a rare disease that might prevent him from serving out a four-year presidential term.

No credible evidence was ever produced to indicate that Johnson was aware of the rumormongering, but there seemed clear evidence that his long-time aide and political manager, John Connally, had approved use of the questionable tactic. In any event, the stratagem failed and the Kennedy-Johnson ticket emerged from the Democratic convention.

During the general-election campaign, the issues of Kennedy's Catholicism and his health were again brought before the voters—this time by the Republicans. In public statements, Republican presidential nominee Richard M. Nixon took a high-minded position on the religious question. He asserted repeatedly that religion was not an issue, but each time he said it new attention was focused on Kennedy's Catholic faith. Meanwhile, hatemongers continued papering the country—particularly in heavily Protestant areas—with anti-Catholic smear literature. At one point, congressional investigators tracking down the sources of such literature found that some of it was being printed by a company whose incorporation papers had been filed by William Casey, a law partner of Republican National Chairman Leonard Hall. Casey claimed he had routinely acted as an attorney for the printing company and that there was no significance to its printing of the smear literature. As for Hall, who had managed Dwight D. Eisenhower's successful presidential campaign in 1956 and was a long-time confidant of Nixon, there was no evidence he was involved in the matter in any way.

As he had in West Virginia, Kennedy again felt obliged to confront the religious issue directly. In a speech before the Houston Ministerial Association in Texas, he pledged to act independently if elected president and said he saw no conflict between his political

59

views and his determination to remain a "good Catholic." His speech was well received and went a long way toward answering the doubts expressed by many sincere non-Catholics.

It is axiomatic in politics that dirty work normally is done by individuals other than the candidate. Then, if a dirty trick backfires, the candidate can deny having anything to do with it. Thus, Nixon attempted—with some success—to continue insisting that the religious issue had no place in the campaign. But others active in his organization never let the issue die. As Nixon himself later pointed out in his book, *Six Crises*, there was a backlash against such tactics. Nixon, in fact, claimed the Kennedy forces helped engender the backlash. Referring to Kennedy's speech before the Houston clergymen, he wrote:

> This very effective speech was recorded on video tape, and it was being played and replayed across the country. . . . [These television showings occurred] far more often in northern cities, where [they] might be expected to appeal to Catholic voters, than in the South and Midwest, where one would expect the heaviest anti-Catholic or simply non-Catholic population. Furthermore, my staff showed me a file of "scare" headlines and news stories from the nation's press.

Among the headlines Nixon cited were:

DEMOCRATS HIT BACK ON RELIGION—*The New York Times*

JACK'S BROTHER [Robert F. Kennedy] SAYS RE-
LIGION TOP ISSUE—*The State*, Columbia, South
Carolina
RELIGIOUS ISSUE STRESSED AT KENNEDY CONFER-
ENCE—*Nashville Banner*
JOHNSON BLASTS "HATERS" ATTACKS ON CATHO-
LICS—*Washington Post*

During the general-election campaign, Kennedy was
accused not only of being dominated by members of
his own religion but also by members of the Jewish
faith. One notorious anti-Semitic hatemonger, the late
Conde McGinley, distributed hundreds of thousands of
posters showing Kennedy standing in front of a group
of leaders of New York's Liberal party. Among those
behind him were several prominent men who, coin-
cidentally, were Jewish. McGinley's posters identified
the men in a caption that read: "Behind Kennedy
Stands the Jew."

Shortly before election day the issue of Kennedy's
health surfaced one last time when a California surgeon
began distributing a letter referring to his well-known
adrenal insufficiency. The letter said Kennedy took
cortisone "to support his adrenal needs." It claimed,
further, that taking cortisone was just about on a par
with heroin addiction. "Such an unreliable, sick man
should not be allowed to assume the responsibility of
national leadership," the letter said.

The Democrats, however, were not blameless during
the 1960 presidential campaign. Former Illinois Governor Adlai E. Stevenson—a two-time Democratic

61

presidential candidate himself—was quoted as "wondering out loud" why no major issue was made of Nixon's religion. Nixon was a Quaker and, as Stevenson pointed out, "many Quakers are pacifists." The remark was out of character for Stevenson, who did as much as any candidate of his generation to elevate the ethical standards of American politics. As he well knew, Nixon was far from a pacifist.

North Carolina Governor Luther Hodges, who would later serve as U.S. secretary of commerce, also commented on Nixon's religion. "We had to choose between a Catholic [Al Smith] and a Quaker [Herbert Hoover] in 1928," he said. "We elected a Quaker and lived to regret it. And, if you vote for a Quaker this time, you will live to regret it horribly." For Hodges as well, the comment was uncharacteristic. A courtly southern gentleman who was extremely popular with some members of the Kennedy organization, he should have been above such a tactic. To attack Nixon's policies was one thing; to attack his religious heritage, while at the same time defending Kennedy's right to be president in spite of his Catholicism, was the worst sort of double-standard politics.

Congressman Adam Clayton Powell, a Baptist minister and controversial figure on Capitol Hill, made reference to a long-time bugaboo in politics—the Ku Klux Klan. A prominent leader of civil rights groups, and a black, Powell had every right to attack the Klan. But he did so in the most demagogic fashion by falsely accusing Nixon of somehow being tied up with the Klan. "The Klan is riding again," he said. "And all bigots will vote for Nixon and all right-thinking Christians and Jews will vote for Kennedy, rather than be found in the ranks of the Klan-minded." Powell went to his grave without ever explaining why he had omitted Buddhists, Mohammedans, agnostics, atheists, or practitioners of other religious or nonreligious beliefs.

The labor movement strongly backed the Kennedy-Johnson ticket, pouring money, manpower, and other resources into the campaign. The Committee on Political Education (COPE) of the American Federation of Labor–Congress of Industrial Organizations (AFL–CIO) resorted to its own hate-literature campaign against Nixon. One COPE pamphlet charged that the campaign was not between Kennedy and Nixon, but rather between "liberty and bigotry." Still another labor committee echoed the claim that a vote for Nixon was a vote for the Ku Klux Klan.

Powell and the labor unions were not the only Democratic forces that brought out the issues of race in an attempt to discredit Nixon's candidacy. In fact, during the 1960 campaign Nixon had the dubious distinction of being smeared in the North on the ground that he discriminated against black people and in the South on the ground that he favored equal rights for them.

Some of those opposing his presidential campaign in the North distributed leaflets containing excerpts from a deed to a Washington house Nixon had bought nine years earlier. The deed contained a clause, known as a "restrictive covenant," barring future sale of the house to a black person. It also barred a resale to "Armenians, Jews, Hebrews and Syrians"—but the emphasis in the leaflets was on blacks. Emblazoned intermittently across the leaflets was the word "Shame!"

Although Nixon obviously should have known better than to sign a deed with such a discriminatory clause, his supporters bitterly assailed the leaflets. They pointed out that the United States Supreme Court had outlawed such restrictive covenants three years before Nixon bought the house. Thus the clause could not have been enforced. Still, Nixon's detractors continued distributing the leaflets.

In the South, where racial discrimination was frequently enforced by law at the time, some of those opposing Nixon's candidacy took a different tack. They distributed other literature showing pictures of Nixon posing in a friendly fashion with blacks. The literature also made the point that Nixon had been a member of the National Association for the Advancement of Colored People (NAACP). The message seemed clear: If elected president, Nixon would try to upset the status quo in the South by helping blacks seek full equality under the law with whites. Under the conditions then prevailing in the South, the literature was calculated to appeal to the racial prejudices of white voters.

Like many candidates for election, both Kennedy and Nixon promised the voters vague and sweeping reforms. Kennedy pitched his campaign on the claim that it was time "to get America moving" again. For example, he asserted that President Dwight D. Eisenhower's Republican administration had permitted the United States to adopt a second-rate military posture and had allowed a so-called missile gap to develop in favor of the Soviet Union.

As he had done throughout his political career, Nixon accused his Democratic opponents during the campaign of being "soft on communism." Such allegations against John F. Kennedy and Lyndon B. Johnson should have been laughable. Both men had long records of anti-communism. Kennedy, in fact, had been accused by liberals of lacking sufficient fervor in opposing the witch-hunt tactics of Senator Joseph McCarthy, the Wisconsin Republican whose investigations of "subversion" had made life miserable for Presidents Truman and Eisenhower.

As a young congressman, Nixon himself had won national attention for his work on the red-baiting House Committee on Un-American Activities (HUAC). He had continued to enjoy support among the nation's most vociferous anticommunist and antiliberal elements while serving in the Senate and as Eisenhower's vice president. Thus it was perhaps natural that he should continue mining the deep vein of American mistrust of the communists. But the manner in which he did so against Kennedy and Johnson was seen by many—including his Democratic opponents—as still another example of dirty politics. Nixon contended that he would "stand up" to the Soviet Union, whereas Kennedy and Johnson would not.

Kennedy, for his part, resorted to tactics that later moved Nixon to accuse him of compromising government secrets. On Eisenhower's orders, Kennedy and Johnson had been given confidential briefings on foreign policy by officials of the State Department and the Central Intelligence Agency (CIA). Among other things, Kennedy learned plans were afoot to provide secret support to anticommunist Cuban exiles seeking the overthrow of Premier Fidel Castro. At the time,

Castro had not yet publicly emerged as a staunch communist. He was a hero to many Cubans and Americans for ousting from power the corrupt regime of right-wing dictator Fulgencio Batista. Although some American experts considered him a communist, others regarded him as a revolutionary whose political doctrine had not yet been determined.

In any event, Kennedy was eager to demonstrate he could be just as anticommunist as Nixon. As a result, he made vigorous anti-Castro speeches that were taken to mean he would offer strong support to the Cuban exile movement—perhaps including even armed intervention against Castro. Nixon, knowing the Eisenhower administration was already secretly planning such intervention, refrained from echoing Kennedy's promises. He would later claim he did so to protect "national security" and that Kennedy's speeches on the subject were "reckless" and compromised the Eisenhower plan's secrecy. Eventually, after Kennedy became president, he put into effect the plan initiated under Eisenhower. A force of Cuban exiles—organized, trained, and equipped by the U.S. Central Intelligence Agency —invaded Cuba but was routed by Castro's troops in the battle of the Bay of Pigs.

The smears and other examples of dirty politics involved in the 1960 presidential campaign affected U.S. campaign practices for years. Tensions between Democratic and Republican leaders increased. In the end, Richard Nixon and his political allies claimed they had been victimized by the Democrats in the 1960 campaign and thus had been forced to retaliate. But these claims seemed to be overstatements and rationalizations. The politics practiced by the Kennedy forces never resembled the illegal acts carried out years later by Nixon and his subordinates, and neither justified nor excused them.

6 THE SMEAR ARTISTS

Early in 1973 Samuel J. Archibald, executive director of a citizens' organization called the Fair Campaign Practices Committee, told news reporters that more examples of dirty politics arose during 1972 than in any year in recent history. He said his organization— a nonpartisan group that had monitored political campaigns since 1954—received 25 percent more complaints in 1972 than in any previous presidential election year. Perhaps more important, Archibald said that Americans were apparently accepting "dirty politics as a way of life."

Yet the smear campaigns and other practices Archibald referred to have been with us since the eighteenth century and have harmed the careers of even such revered figures as George Washington, Thomas Jefferson, and Abraham Lincoln.

Although schoolchildren are taught that George Washington was a beloved figure who supposedly could not tell a lie, that was not the picture of the first president painted by some of his contemporaries. Washington was subjected to vicious smear campaigns throughout his presidency. Swept into office by a unanimous vote of the electoral college, with the widespread support of a newly independent citizenry, he might have expected to enjoy relative freedom from criticism. Instead, his motives were often distorted and his policies derided by political enemies determined to advance their own careers at all costs.

It was said that Washington, having led the war to free the American people from allegiance to the British crown, now wanted to be king himself. Such a charge would eventually be leveled, as well, against several succeeding presidents. But it seemed particularly misplaced when directed at Washington, since he fought as president against the views of some advisers who truly did favor ultimate development of an American royal family. Some of those who did not describe Washington as an American royalist did sometimes accuse him of retaining undue fondness for the British. It was a rare day when he was not accused of some sort of heinous double cross of the American people.

Tom Paine, the revolutionary pamphleteer and author of *Common Sense*, accused Washington of being "treacherous in private friendship and a hypocrite in public life." And, compared with some other allegations against Washington, Paine's words were mild.

69

Oliver Wolcott, who served as the nation's second secretary of the treasury, wrote that the smear campaign against Washington was so bitter it would "debase the character of an angel."

Washington's immediate successors fared little better with the smear artists. His vice president, John Adams, who became the second president, was falsely accused of being both pro-British and pro-French. In the 1796 presidential campaign, newspapers supporting Thomas Jefferson spread malicious stories about Adams, some based on half-truths and others totally fabricated. The most blatant lie of the campaign was published by a Boston newspaper, the *Independent Chronicle*, which claimed that Adams had secretly tried to force Washington's ouster as commander of American military forces during the Revolution. Actually, Adams had stood squarely behind Washington's leadership.

Meanwhile, Thomas Jefferson was subjected to equally false and malicious smears. Some of his political enemies accused him of everything from alcoholism to fathering illegitimate children by slaves on his plantation.

A smear campaign also marred the 1844 presidential election between James K. Polk and Henry Clay. Just before the election, a newspaper in Ithaca, New York, published a supposed excerpt from the journal of someone calling himself Baron Roorback. In *Roorback's Tour Through the Western and Southern States in 1836*, the author claimed he had attended an auction where Polk had bought forty-three slaves. Roorback described in detail how a branding iron had been used to burn Polk's initials on the shoulders of the slaves.

Other anti-Polk newspapers quickly picked up and reprinted this story of inhumane treatment. But the smear came so late in the campaign that Polk had no chance to refute it; although he won the election, the libel cut heavily into his vote. Later, it was revealed that the entire story was false.

However, the incident added a word to the American political language. Ever since, the term "roorback" has been used to describe any false or damaging story about a politician issued so late in a campaign that he has no opportunity for an effective rebuttal.

Twenty years after the Polk-Clay campaign, President Abraham Lincoln was subjected to vicious smears when he sought re-election. He was called everything from a fiend, ghoul, and lunatic to murderer, robber, and traitor. His wife, at the height of the Civil War, was accused of being a Confederate sympathizer. Some went as far as to call her a spy. The stories became so widespread that Lincoln felt compelled to issue a denial, saying: "I, Abraham Lincoln, President of the United States . . . know that it is untrue that any of my family hold treasonable communication with the enemy." Lincoln won re-election but was assassinated before completing his term.

In 1884 the presidential campaign between Grover Cleveland and James G. Blaine involved smears on both sides. Cleveland was accused of being a drunkard and the father of an illegitimate child. A bachelor, he admitted sexual intimacy with a widow who was his frequent companion, but he denied allegations that he had fathered an illegitimate child by her. Nonetheless, his Republican opponents pilloried him constantly on

71

the matter. Some pushed baby carriages with signs that made disparaging comments about the supposed illegitimate child. Others chanted: "Ma, Ma, where's my Pa? Gone to the White House, ha, ha, ha!"

The Democrats, for their part, falsely accused Blaine of financial irregularities. And they had a chant of their own: "Blaine, Blaine, James G. Blaine. The continental liar from the state of Maine!"

The 1884 campaign was also notorious for the injection of a religious issue. In Blaine's presence, a Protestant clergyman denounced the Democrats—describing them as members of a party "whose antecedents are Rum, Romanism and Rebellion." Rum and rebellion were serious enough words, but the use of Romanism—a reference to supposed influence on the party by the Roman Catholic church—was too much for many voters. When Blaine declined to repudiate the clergyman's allegations, there was an outcry from Catholic voters. Many Catholics who previously had leaned toward Blaine voted against him, helping ensure Cleveland's victory.

One of the most celebrated smear campaigns of relatively recent vintage occurred during the 1950 Democratic primary for a U.S. Senate seat in Florida. It was conducted on two levels—one humorous and the other far from it.

The opponents in the race were the incumbent senator, Claude Pepper, and his challenger, Congressman George Smathers. In speeches to the more sophisticated urban audiences, Smathers accused Pepper—falsely—of being procommunist. He even went as far as to label his opponent "Red Pepper." The primary campaign took place during a period of anticommunist hysteria, and Smathers's name calling took a heavy toll.

In a less serious vein, the second level of Smathers's smear campaign involved speeches to unsophisticated rural voters in which he described Pepper in unfamiliar words that, while entirely innocent, had a scandalous ring to them. Smathers spelled out for the rural voters a list of what sounded like deep, dark secrets from Pepper's family closet. For one thing, Smathers said, Pepper had been described as a well-known sexagenarian. There was no telling what the voters thought the word meant, although it merely means a person who is past the age of sixty. Similarly, Smathers announced to shocked audiences that Pepper had a sister who had gone to New York and become a thespian. A thespian sounded sinister to the unsophisticated audience, but all it means is an actress. Smathers also charged that Pepper's brother was a practicing *Homo sapiens*—which was mistaken by some for homosexual but means merely a modern human being. Not only that, Smathers said, but when Pepper was a college student, he had been known to matriculate. Heaven knows what the rural voters thought that word meant!

The clever two-level smear campaign by Smathers worked to perfection. He defeated Pepper in the primary and went on to win the general election. Pepper never returned to the Senate, but later he did win a seat in the House.

Smathers was far from alone in using smear techniques that involved allegations of procommunist tendencies. For years, candidates and their campaign organizations had tarred their opponents with such

73

words as "commie," "Red," and "pinko." The most celebrated political witch-hunter in the nation's history was the late Senator Joseph McCarthy of Wisconsin. McCarthy, a Republican with a mediocre record, was almost unknown on the national scene until he suddenly seized on the issue of "communists in government" in 1950.

As chairman of a Senate investigating committee, McCarthy smeared the names of countless Americans —both public officials and private citizens. In addition, he intervened in numerous election campaigns outside his home state, leveling smear allegations at politicians who had criticized his witch-hunting activities.

Shortly after launching his so-called "anti-communist crusade," McCarthy intruded upon the 1950 Maryland campaign for a seat in the U.S. Senate. Senator Millard Tydings, a Democrat, was up for re-election. Tydings had served in the Senate for twenty-four years—longer than all but two of his colleagues—and was seeking another six-year term. Far from a left-winger, he was so conservative that the late President Franklin D. Roosevelt had once tried to purge him from the Senate for opposing his liberal New Deal programs. Now, McCarthy was seeking his defeat with the unlikely claim that Tydings was, of all things, a communist sympathizer.

Tydings had incurred McCarthy's wrath while serving as chairman of a special Senate subcommittee assigned to investigate McCarthy's charges that the State Department had been infiltrated by communists. In typical fashion, McCarthy had produced few, if any, facts to document his allegations.

74

When the Tydings subcommittee completed its investigation, it issued a report condemning McCarthy in some of the sharpest language ever used by senators to describe one of their colleagues:

We are constrained fearlessly and frankly to call the [McCarthy] charges, and the methods employed to give them ostensible validity, what they truly are—a fraud and a hoax perpetrated on the Senate of the United States and the American people. They represent perhaps the most nefarious campaign of half-truths and untruths in the history of this Republic. For the first time in our history, we have seen the totalitarian technique of the "big lie" employed on a sustained basis.

In retaliation, McCarthy vowed to bring about Tydings's defeat in his Maryland re-election campaign. To do so, he launched a smear campaign rarely matched in the annals of American politics. The high point of the campaign came when McCarthy and his allies distributed hundreds of thousands of copies of a tabloid newspaper featuring a faked photograph (made by cropping and pasting two photos) that depicted Tydings standing beside and apparently listening attentively to American Communist party leader Earl Browder. The picture caption read "Communist leader Earl Browder, shown at left in this composite picture, was a star witness at the Tydings committee hearings, and was cajoled into saying Owen Lattimore and others accused of disloyalty were not communists. . . ."

The tabloid containing the photograph and other

tactics used by McCarthy and his backers accomplished their purpose. When the ballots were counted, Tydings lost his Senate seat by 43,000 votes to the first Maryland Republican elected to the Senate in twenty-two years.

Richard Nixon was another politician who rose to power by making allegations of communist sympathy against his opponents. In his first election campaign in 1946, Nixon ran for Congress in the Twelfth District of California. The district had traditionally been Republican over the years but had nonetheless elected a Democrat, Jerry Voorhis, to five consecutive terms in Congress. Voorhis, who was seeking re-election, was generally regarded as a liberal. Nixon, however, set out to persuade the electorate that his opponent was nothing less than a tool of the communist rulers of the Soviet Union.

Pledging in advance of the congressional race to wage a "fighting, rocking, socking campaign," Nixon quickly made clear he would keep the promise. In particular, Nixon charged that Voorhis was controlled by the Political Action Committee (PAC) of the Congress of Industrial Organizations, one of the two major labor organizations that later merged to produce the AFL–CIO.

PAC had supported the candidacies of many leading politicians, including Presidents Franklin D. Roosevelt and Harry S Truman. But Nixon tried to make it appear that PAC was an enemy of free enterprise and virtually equivalent to the Soviet Union. Three days before the election, Nixon's headquarters released a statement accusing Voorhis of "consistently voting the

Moscow-PAC line in Congress." The statement went on to attack "the insolence of Moscow in telling the American voters to elect PAC candidates, such as Mr. Voorhis." It concluded by saying Nixon was "a man who will talk American and at the same time vote American in Congress . . . and fight in and out of Congress to perpetuate American ideals and American freedom."

Nixon's message was clear: He represented true Americanism, whereas Voorhis represented un-Americanism. And Nixon's strategy worked to perfection: when the votes were tallied, he had 65,586 while Voorhis had 49,994.

Four years later, Nixon ran for a seat in the Senate and used similar tactics against his opponent, Democratic Congresswoman Helen Gahagan Douglas. Mrs. Douglas, who had been an actress before serving three terms in Congress, had a reputation as a vigorous anticommunist. Nonetheless, Nixon pitched his campaign on allegations that she had somehow been sympathetic to the Communist Party line. In an early speech, he said, "It just so happens that my opponent is a member of a small clique which joins the notorious Communist party-liner, [Congressman] Vito Marcantonio of New York, in voting time after time against measures that are for the security of this country."

To promote the idea that Mrs. Douglas was a "pinko," Nixon began calling her the "Pink Lady." His campaign organization distributed 550,000 campaign leaflets—printed on bright pink paper—that purported to show similarities between her voting record and that of the alleged communist, Marcantonio. Again, his smear tactics worked. He defeated Mrs. Douglas by 680,000 votes and continued on the road that would lead him to the vice-presidency and ultimately to the White House.

When Democrat Lyndon Johnson ran against Republican Barry Goldwater in the 1964 presidential campaign, smear mongers on both sides had a field day.

Throughout the country, Goldwater campaign headquarters distributed flyers claiming that Johnson was backed by the communists. They also promoted the sale of a paperback book, *A Texan Looks at Lyndon*, by J. Evetts Haley, that accused Johnson of being a completely unscrupulous politician.

One of the most distasteful episodes of the 1964 campaign concerned the arrest of a key Johnson aide, Walter Jenkins, on a disorderly conduct charge in a Washington YMCA men's room known to the police as a hangout for homosexuals. The arrest was made about a month before the election. Jenkins, who had been a respected aide to Johnson for years on Capitol Hill and at the White House, was accused of homosexual conduct. The press did not become immediately aware of the incident.

But then anonymous tipsters began telephoning the news media with information about the case. When reporters checked on the information, they found entries on the police blotter referring to the arrest. Two attorneys who were close friends of both Johnson and Jenkins, Abe Fortas (later appointed to the Supreme Court) and Clark Clifford (later appointed secretary of defense), appealed privately to the news media not to publish the story. They argued that publicity about the arrest could destroy the life of a man who had been a dedicated public servant and devoted husband and father. The news media agreed to hold off publication of the story at least temporarily.

Meanwhile, Jenkins entered a hospital. His physician said he was suffering from nervous exhaustion. Several days after the arrest—while the news media were continuing to hold the story—Republican National Chairman Dean Burch issued a statement referring to a "report sweeping Washington that the White House is desperately trying to suppress a major news story affecting the national security." While Burch did not spell out in detail what the story was, the news media almost immediately made public the details of the Jenkins case.

Burch's action, in itself, did not constitute a political smear. He probably overstated the case in claiming the White House was trying to suppress "a major news story affecting the national security." The premise was that Jenkins, who was privy to numerous White House secrets, might be subject to blackmail over the arrest and that national security might somehow be compromised. Still, overstatement or not, it did seem that the public was entitled to the facts of the case—much as they might embarrass Jenkins, his family, and the entire Johnson camp. Once the story came out, Jenkins resigned and Johnson announced that he had accepted the resignation with regret.

Some of the events that followed, however, did represent full-blown political smears. Offensive literature swept the country, leaving the impression that homosexuality had been permitted to run rampant in the Johnson White House. In California, among other places, Goldwater backers distributed bumper stickers reading, JOHNSON IS KING AND JENKINS IS QUEEN. At a Goldwater banquet in Louisiana, a political leader handed out supposed three-dollar bills that he claimed were good for "three bucks at Jenkins House."

At the same time, Republicans charged that their presidential candidate had been subjected to more than his share of smear attacks. Throughout the campaign, the Democrats had been trying to depict Goldwater as irresponsible—a supposed "shoot-from-the-hip" candidate who might destroy the Social Security system and turn the Tennessee Valley Authority (TVA—an important source of inexpensive, public electric power) over to private ownership.

The Republicans were particularly incensed over a series of television commercials aired nationally by President Johnson's campaign organization. Several of the commercials struck hard at the theme that Goldwater, if elected president, might bring about a nuclear holocaust. The Democrats maintained the commercials were justified on the ground that Goldwater had advocated using nuclear bombs in the Vietnam war. But the Republicans claimed that was a distortion of his position. At the time, communist forces were using the thick foliage of Vietnamese jungles as protective cover to disguise their movements from American warplanes passing overhead. Goldwater suggested that low-yield atomic weapons could be used to defoliate the jungles, thus depriving the communists of their cover. But his backers insisted he had never come right out and advocated such a policy—that he had merely suggested it as a possibility and had added that he did not think it would ever come to pass.

The Democrats, however, made no such distinction in their television commercials. One commercial showed a small girl picking petals from a daisy in a beautiful meadow. As she did, she counted: "One, two, three, four, five, six, seven, eight, nine, ten." Suddenly, at the count of ten, a man's voice could be heard drowning out the girl's. He was counting in reverse order, in the manner of a nuclear countdown: "Ten, nine, eight, seven, six, five, four, three, two, one, zero."

At zero, the television screen went black. A nuclear explosion was simulated. The little girl was blown up; the familiar shape of a mushroom cloud filled the screen. In the background could be heard the voice of President Johnson, delivering an ominous message: "These are the stakes—to make a world in which all of God's children can live or to go into the dark. We must either love each other or we must die."

Again, the screen went black for a moment. A line then appeared urging viewers to vote for Johnson while a background voice commented: "The stakes are too high for you to stay home."

Republican National Chairman Burch complained that such commercials falsely depicted Goldwater's positions, making him appear irresponsible with atomic weapons. Not only his fellow Republicans, but numerous Democrats as well, agreed. Many viewers from both parties telephoned and wrote television stations carrying the commercials and the Democratic National Committee to protest what they regarded as a vicious smear of Goldwater.

Democratic National Chairman John Bailey denied the commercials misrepresented Goldwater's positions. He argued that they dramatically conveyed to the public an image Goldwater himself had established. Nonetheless, without fanfare, the Democrats stopped showing the controversial commercials a short time later. But by that time, in the view of Goldwater's adherents, the damage had already been done.

7 THE FAIR CAMPAIGN PRACTICES COMMITTEE

For more than two decades, an organization called the Fair Campaign Practices Committee has been trying to eliminate smears and other unsavory tactics from American political campaigns. The committee is a private group and is limited by a lack of enforcement powers, but it has had a measure of success in fulfilling its mandate.

During the early 1950s there was a rash of particularly rough political campaigns. The 1950 congressional elections, for example, included so many smear campaigns that the *New York Times* was prompted to publish an editorial reading in part:

If this sort of thing continues, it will become increasingly difficult to get decent men and women to stand for public office because of the unjusti-

83

fied abuse suffered en route. . . . When almost
everyone is calling everybody else a liar and thief,
the result becomes a standoff. There is, then, no
black and white of reputation in the public mind,
only a muddy gray.

Several congressional committees studied the problem and suggested a variety of remedies. One of them,
proposed by a Senate elections subcommittee headed
by Guy Gillette of Iowa, was the establishment of "a
continuing committee of eminent members of both
parties, working jointly for higher and cleaner standards
of campaigning." The Senate subcommittee said creation of such a nonpartisan panel could do as much as
the enactment of new legislation "to rid this nation of
abuses which are reaching alarming proportions."

When the Fair Campaign Practices Committee was
organized late in 1954, attorney Charles P. Taft of
Cincinnati, son of the late President William Howard
Taft and brother of Republican Senator Robert Taft,
was named chairman. Bruce L. Felknor, a former
newspaperman and public relations executive, became
executive director. Felknor later wrote an extremely
valuable book describing the work of the committee
and the long history of shoddy campaign practices in
the United States.

Announcement of the committee's formation was
made at a Washington press conference attended by
numerous prominent political figures, including Democratic National Chairman Stephen Mitchell and Republican National Chairman Leonard Hall. Both chairmen took the occasion to sign and endorse a code of

fair campaign practices drawn up by the new committee, whose members included Anna Lord Strauss of New York, immediate past president of the League of Women Voters of the United States; Barry Bingham, publisher of the *Louisville Times* and *Courier-Journal*; and Palmer Hoyt, publisher of the *Denver Post*. Copies of the code were mailed to all candidates running for the House and Senate in the 1954 elections. The candidates were asked to make public pledges to abide by the code and to signify their support by mailing signed copies of the code to the committee. The code read as follows:

There are basic principles of decency, honesty and fair play which every candidate for public office in the United States has a moral obligation to observe and uphold, in order that, after vigorously contested but fairly conducted campaigns, our citizens may exercise their constitutional right to free and untrammeled choice and the will of the people may be fully and clearly expressed on the issues before the country.

Therefore:

I shall conduct my campaign in the best American tradition, discussing the issues as I see them, presenting my record and policies with sincerity and frankness, and criticizing without fear or favor the record and policies of my opponent and his party which merit criticism.

I shall defend and uphold the right of every qualified American voter to full and equal participation in the electoral process.

85

I shall condemn the use of personal vilification, character defamation, whispering campaigns, libel, slander or scurrilous attacks on any candidate or his personal or family life.

I shall condemn the use of campaign material of any sort which misrepresents, distorts or otherwise falsifies the facts regarding any candidate, as well as the use of malicious or unfounded accusations against any candidate which aim at creating or exploiting doubts, without justification, as to his loyalty and patriotism.

I shall condemn any appeal to prejudice based on race, creed or national origin.

I shall condemn any dishonest or unethical practice which tends to corrupt or undermine our American system of free elections or which hampers or prevents the full and free expression of the will of the voters.

I shall immediately and publicly repudiate support deriving from any individual or group which resorts, on behalf of my candidacy, to the methods and tactics which I condemn.

In some cases, pressure from the committee has succeeded in preventing campaign abuses. During the 1964 Johnson-Goldwater campaign, for example, the committee learned in advance that the Goldwater camp was preparing a highly inflammatory film for showing on network television. The film, *Choice*, showed example after example of the seamy side of American life— stripteasers, pornographic literature, narcotics addicts —as well as numerous scenes in which blacks were seen rioting and looting store windows. The implication was that President Johnson was responsible for such conditions and that only a vote for Goldwater could remedy them.

An attempt was made by the Goldwater campaign organization to mislead the public by saying the film was being sponsored by a group calling itself Mothers for a Moral America, which was supposedly independent and nonpolitical. Actually, Mothers for a Moral America was a front group established by the Goldwater organization.

The Democrats learned about the existence of the film and obtained a copy before it was to be shown on television. They arranged a screening for members of the press and the Fair Campaign Practices Committee. The committee issued a challenge to Goldwater's organization, which continued to deny any connection with the film, either to accept responsibility for it or abandon it. Finally, Goldwater—who had not yet seen the film—viewed it himself. He decided it was "racist" and ordered that it not be shown on television. The committee's action unquestionably played a role in sparing the public from exposure to that particular political smear.

The committee also took up the cudgels on Goldwater's behalf when he was subjected during the same campaign to what many regarded as a political smear passed off as a poll of psychiatrists on his mental fitness for the presidency. The poll was conducted by a magazine called *Fact*, published by Ralph Ginzburg.

Ginzburg had obtained a mailing list of more than 12,000 psychiatrists across the country. He had sent them a questionnaire asking their opinions on whether Goldwater was psychologically fit to serve as president. None of the psychiatrists had ever examined Goldwater. Yet more than 1,700 of them replied to the questionnaire. And of those, almost 1,200 said they considered Goldwater psychologically unfit for the presidency.

About a month before the election, Ginzburg published the results of the poll. He quoted from the letters sent by the psychiatrists—some of which described Goldwater in such terms as "schizophrenic," "paranoid," and "adolescent." Publication of the results of the poll touched off storms of controversy in both the political and medical worlds. Ginzburg and the psychiatrists who had participated were roundly criticized by medical organizations and by both backers and opponents of Goldwater's campaign.

The Fair Campaign Practices Committee quickly stepped into the case amid reports that the Democratic party had secretly financed the poll. The committee found no evidence to support such reports. It served a valuable function in coordinating and releasing to the public an effective response to the *Fact* article, including critical statements from responsible medical officials and spokesmen for both the Democratic and Republican parties. Among those quoted in a report issued by the committee was Democratic National Chairman Bailey, who not only emphasized his party's refusal to make any political use of the poll but also charged that "the long-distance analysis of any candidate by questionnaire is not responsible journalism."

Periodically, the committee is called upon for advice by candidates who feel their opponents are distorting their records. One such case occurred in 1962 when a two-term Republican congressman, Leonard Halpern of New York, was running for re-election. He was opposed in the campaign by a relatively inexperienced Democratic candidate, Leonard Finz. The Democratic Congressional Campaign Committee had supplied Finz with potential campaign ammunition in the form of a report on Halpern's legislative record since entering Congress. The report reflected that, although Halpern had introduced more than 300 bills in Congress, none of any broad consequence had ever been enacted into law. Finz thus branded Halpern in his campaign as a "do-nothing" congressman and referred to the record as proof.

But the record did not tell the whole story. Since Halpern was a Republican in a Democratic-controlled Congress, he stood little chance of getting a bill under his own name pushed through the House. The Democrats, seeking credit for their own party, could usually see to it that only bills sponsored by their own party members were passed. Under House rules, however, all congressmen who agreed on the merits of a piece of legislation could introduce identical bills. Halpern thus had seen bills identical to his own—but bearing Democratic congressmen's names—enacted into law. In some cases, he had helped push such measures through the House.

In his book, Bruce Felknor described how committee staff members had discovered while interviewing Halpern that President Kennedy, although a Democrat, had given the Republican congressman six pens he had used in signing various bills into law. The pens

89

had been intended as tokens of appreciation for Halpern's help in obtaining Republican support for the bills. As Felknor put it: "There was the answer; Halpern had been too close to the problem [to see it]. He returned to the campaign, summoned a press conference, told the story and brandished the six pens from the Democratic president—and won the election by a substantially greater margin than his election in 1960."

The same year that the Halpern affair occurred, the Fair Campaign Practices Committee helped dissuade Democrats from using below-the-belt tactics in another campaign. Nelson Rockefeller, then the Republican governor of New York, was seeking re-election. He had just been divorced from his first wife, and there was speculation on how his marital troubles would affect the campaign. Rockefeller's Democratic opponent— Robert Morgenthau, the former United States attorney in New York—scrupulously refused to be drawn into discussions of the matter. But officials of the Women's Division of the Democratic State Committee tried to make political capital out of the divorce case.

They ordered preparation of a large advertisement, to be published in newspapers throughout the state, bearing the headline WOMEN DON'T WANT A PART-TIME GOVERNOR ANY MORE THAN THEY WANT A PART-TIME HUSBAND. The prospective ad said that Rockefeller, who had made no secret of his interest in seeking the Republican presidential nomination, was so busy "romancing the White House" that he neglected his gubernatorial duties. Use of such language was clearly intended to remind the public of Rockefeller's matrimonial troubles. If any further emphasis were needed,

90

the ad also included a picture of Democratic candidate Morgenthau and his entire family—making the point that he was at home, where he belonged, while Rockefeller was presumably neglecting both family and official responsibilities.

Before the Democratic Women's Division actually bought ad space, the ad copy was brought to the attention of a high party official. He recognized it for what it was—a low blow in a campaign that candidate Morgenthau had thus far taken pains to keep on a high plane. The party official thought publication of the advertisement, in addition to being unscrupulous, would be politically stupid—that it would bring a backlash of voter resentment against Morgenthau. He tried to persuade leaders of the Women's Division to abandon plans for publishing the ad, but they remained committed to the original scheme.

The party official then asked the Fair Campaign Practices Committee for an evaluation of the potential results of the ad's publication. Committee staff members told him they were sure Republicans would protest bitterly that such an ad was a dirty trick and that the result would be to touch off a wave of voter reaction against Morgenthau. With that assessment as a major arguing point, the party official went back to the Women's Division leaders and made a new appeal for abandonment of the ad. He finally persuaded them that the committee was right. As a result, the ad was never published.

Rockefeller, who had been heavily favored throughout the campaign, went on to win the election. But Morgenthau emerged with his reputation for integrity intact. He later was elected district attorney of New York County (Manhattan)—one of the most prestigious prosecutor's jobs in the nation.

Without question, the work of the Fair Campaign Practices Committee has curbed some of the seamier techniques of political campaigns. But the committee's capacity to produce a higher level of campaigning is limited by its lack of enforcement power and its relatively small budget and staff. Governmental efforts to regulate political campaigns have likewise had limited success, partly due to elected officials' reluctance to police their own ranks and partly due to concentration on restricted areas of reform such as finance laws. The murkiest area—the one in which there is perhaps the least likelihood of true reform—is the political smear.

This country's tradition of protecting free speech tends to permit politicians to get away with saying almost anything within reason about their opponents. Libel and slander laws, which ordinarily protect private citizens against being victimized by false written or verbal statements, are of almost no use to political figures. Numerous court decisions over the last two decades have held that public figures such as entertainers and politicians are fair game for virtually anything an opponent or critic writes or says about them. Under these decisions, it is necessary for a public figure who wants to collect damages for libel or slander to prove that the person who wrote or uttered the false statement knew at the time it was false, made no effort to determine its truth, or showed reckless disregard for accuracy and, besides all that, intended malice toward the victim. Such conditions are almost impossible to meet. Thus, in many cases, politicians are forced to hear or read vicious, untrue comments about themselves, shrug their shoulders, and respond, in effect, "that's politics."

President Jimmy Carter was placed in just such a position while he was seeking his party's presidential nomination in early 1976. Although he had been little known nationally at the outset of his campaign, Carter had quickly jumped into a front-runner's position for the Democratic nomination. On January 19, in the year's first test of strength among presidential candidates, Carter made an impressive showing in precinct caucuses that began the process of choosing delegates to the Democratic national convention. A month later, he won an even more significant victory by leading the field in the New Hampshire primary—traditionally the first presidential primary election.

Carter suddenly became a focus of national attention. Rumblings in the news media said that some other candidate would have to stop him—and quickly—or his campaign might build sufficient momentum to carry him all the way to the White House. The next important primary would come in Massachusetts only a week after the New Hampshire vote.

Carter knew the Massachusetts campaign would be rough. All the other candidates—including Senator Henry (Scoop) Jackson of Washington, Congressman Morris (Mo) Udall of Arizona, Alabama Governor George Wallace, and former Peace Corps Director Sargent Shriver—would be attacking him. But Carter never guessed just how rough it could be.

When he arrived in Massachusetts to campaign, fresh

93

from the New Hampshire triumph, he found the state blanketed with smear literature accusing him of all manner of political and personal wrongdoing. The most vicious charged him with somehow being involved in a cover-up of a major narcotics-smuggling operation in Georgia. It claimed that a man described as one of Carter's "key aides" was under investigation as a participant in the drug operation. Carter, it was said, had exerted covert pressure to kill the investigation.

If true, of course, the allegation could have knocked Carter out of the presidential race, but there was no supporting evidence. Indeed, it seemed to be the result of a desperate maneuver on someone's part to discredit Carter before his campaign could build further momentum.

At first, Carter tried to ignore the smear literature. But it kept turning up in every Massachusetts city and town where he campaigned. Reporters began asking him about it.

Finally, on the weekend before the Massachusetts primary, Carter felt obliged to answer the attack. In response to reporters' questions, he said the allegations about the supposed narcotics cover-up were totally false. He knew nothing about any such case, he said. What was more, he denied even knowing the man identified in the smear literature as one of his "key aides."

If Carter was telling the truth—and nobody ever stepped forward to dispute his word—the story told in the smear literature was either completely invented or bore so little resemblance to the truth that it might as well have been. Still, the very news stories that carried Carter's denials gave the smears wider distribution. It is axiomatic that denials rarely catch up with accusations in the news media.

Thus, as the Massachusetts voters went to the polls, at least some of them undoubtedly carried with them doubts about Carter's purported role in the narcotics affair. It seemed clear that Carter's campaign had been hurt; when the votes were counted, he finished well behind Senator Jackson.

Carter never learned who had been responsible for distributing the smear literature. Rumors that the campaign organizations of one or more of his opponents might have been involved were never proved. To his credit, Carter refrained from making the campaign even dirtier by accusing his opponents without evidence. In the end, he was nominated on the first ballot at the Democratic convention and defeated incumbent Gerald Ford in the general election.

The Carter–Ford campaign was hard fought but ended with both men displaying mutual respect. Many observers complained that the presidential campaign had been dull and had lacked meaningful discussions of substantive issues. But at least Ford and Carter had not stooped to indulging in a mud-slinging contest. That is not to say that dirty politics disappeared in 1976—far from it, as the attempted smears of Carter during the primary season attested. Perhaps in reaction to the disgust of many voters with Watergate-era revelations, however, most campaigns sought to avoid out-and-out political smears that might backfire.

It should be emphasized that tough politics need not be dirty politics. Serious discussion of issues, in view

95

of human nature and the egotism of many politicians, often creates situations in which one candidate or another "loses his cool." That can be a healthy exercise. Americans want their political leaders to act as human beings, not automatons. They want to see them laugh, explode in anger, and show the normal reactions appropriate to their activities. Also, they want to be able to judge how well the candidates stand up to stress.

Thus few political experts advocate a system in which campaigns would become bland affairs that bore the electorate to tears. Too many campaigns are dull. There is a place in American politics for humor, for sarcasm, even for pranks.

But a line must be drawn between aggressive politics—what Richard Nixon liked to call "hardball politics"—and dirty politics. That line may perhaps seem fuzzy at times. It can, however, indeed be drawn.

8 A PROFESSIONAL POLITICAL PRANKSTER

On September 26, 1973, at the height of the Watergate furor, a Senate committee investigating the scandal called Patrick J. Buchanan to the witness chair. A former newspaperman, Buchanan served as an influential political adviser and speech writer for President Richard M. Nixon. Although he was one of Nixon's staunchest defenders and one of the administration's strongest advocates of the so-called hardball political technique, there was never any suggestion that he had been directly involved in the various criminal acts committed as part of the Watergate burglary or cover-up. His testimony was intended, instead, to help the committee define for itself and the public the difference between tough, clean politics and dirty politics.

Buchanan was an aggressive witness and did his best

97

to defend the Nixon administration. It was a hopeless task. For by that time there was no question that Watergate had gone far beyond the pale of law. But in discussing the political climate that produced Watergate, Buchanan pointed out that the Republicans felt justified in retaliating for what they considered years of torment at the hands of a Democratic political operative named Richard Tuck.

Asked what tactics he would be willing to use to win a political campaign, Buchanan replied: "Anything that was not immoral, unethical, illegal, or unprecedented in previous Democratic campaigns." While senators and spectators laughed at the remark, Buchanan plunged ahead: "As you know, Mr. Richard [Dick] Tuck is the well-known Democratic prankster. We enjoyed some of his tricks against us as well as, I am sure, he did. Some of the things done to us [by Tuck] were hilarious." As a result, Buchanan said, the Republicans decided to retaliate. And that, he claimed, was one of the reasons for development of a team within the Nixon administration and re-election campaign committee capable of various and sundry activities ultimately labeled as examples of dirty politics.

In an effort to draw the line between tough, clean politics and dirty politics, it seems appropriate at this juncture to examine, among other things, the techniques of Dick Tuck. Although the Republicans tried to excuse Watergate simply as their own version of a Tuck caper, veteran political observers disputed their reasoning. Tuck was a prankster, they said. He was clever, and some of his stunts were indeed hilarious. But they never strayed so far as to represent examples of dirty politics.

Tuck, who received a degree from the University of California in public administration, had turned into the foremost political prankster in the country during the 1950s. At first, it seemed, he pulled his stunts merely for his own amusement. But as he grew more imaginative and competent, his services came into demand from political professionals. Tuck picked Richard Nixon as an early target. And although he served as a hired gun of sorts against other candidates, Tuck continued to find particular delight in developing new ways to embarrass Nixon.

During the 1960 presidential campaign, for example, Tuck seized upon a political issue that had been plaguing Nixon. It involved a controversial loan made by billionaire industrialist Howard Hughes to a brother of Nixon's. Since Nixon was vice president at the time and Hughes's corporate empire profited heavily from government contracts, there were allegations that the loan to Nixon's brother had resulted from political favoritism shown the Hughes empire by the administration. Nixon emphatically denied any impropriety, claiming the loan was unrelated either to him or to any deals between Hughes and the government. The Democrats, however, continued to charge otherwise.

In the midst of the uproar, Nixon appeared at a rally in the Chinatown section of Los Angeles. Tacked to the speaking platform was a sign printed half in English and half in Chinese. The English caption read, WEL- COME NIXON. Before leaving the rally, a beaming Nixon posed for pictures alongside the sign. He did not learn until the pictures appeared in newspapers across the country that the Chinese characters read, WHAT ABOUT

THE HUGHES LOAN? Dick Tuck had gotten a Chinese-American sign painter to prepare the placard and then plant it on the rally platform.

After Nixon lost the 1960 presidential election to John F. Kennedy, he moved back to California. In 1962 he ran for governor against the Democratic incumbent, Edmund (Pat) Brown.

During the campaign, Nixon conducted a so-called whistle-stop tour of California. The train would pull out of one city, roll on to the next, and following time-honored political tradition, Nixon would stand on a platform on the last railroad car to deliver almost the identical speech at each stop. Reporters covering the campaign tired of hearing the speech. Invariably, it would build up to a thunderous climax intended to persuade voters that only a Nixon administration could save California from disaster.

When the train pulled into San Luis Obispo one day, a man carrying a trainman's lantern and wearing a railroad uniform unexpectedly signaled the engineer to pull out of the station. A large crowd was gathered to hear Nixon, but as he stepped onto the rear platform the train began leaving. It was hard to tell who was more surprised—Nixon or the spectators—as he was whisked away without having a chance to deliver the speech. Frantic Nixon aides demanded an explanation from the train's engineer. He told them he had been given the signal to pull away from the station. An investigation revealed, after much confusion, that the trainman giving the signal had been Dick Tuck in disguise.

Campaign trains seemed to hold a special fascination

for Tuck. In 1964 when President Lyndon Johnson was running against Senator Barry Goldwater, Tuck planted an "undercover agent" aboard Goldwater's cross-country campaign special. The agent was a pretty, twenty-three-year-old advertising copy writer named Moira O'Connor, who had been working as a volunteer at the Democratic National Committee headquarters in Washington. Posing as a free-lance magazine writer, she obtained press credentials entitling her to ride the Goldwater Special coast to coast.

Soon after the trip began, bona fide political reporters found under their compartment doors copies of a newspaper called *The Whistle Stop* that mercilessly ridiculed the Goldwater campaign. Tuck had produced several issues of the paper and managed to smuggle them aboard the train with Miss O'Connor.

The first issue said the paper was intended to keep the reporters "advised, informed, protected and, with considerable help from the senator himself [Goldwater], amused." It promised that a second issue would be delivered before breakfast the next day.

At five o'clock the next morning, Goldwater's assistant press secretary, Vic Gold (who would later serve as press secretary to Nixon's first vice president, Spiro T. Agnew), began searching the train for the Democratic "spy" and for copies of the next issue of *The Whistle Stop*. In a supposedly vacant compartment, he found several suitcases filled with copies of the second issue of the newspaper. It claimed a scoop on how Goldwater planned to avoid confusion about the time as the train proceeded west into the central time zone: "The senator has decided to use Washington time—

101

George Washington, that is." The joke was in keeping with numerous 1964 wisecracks accusing Goldwater of being so conservative that he was living in a past century. One joke, which Goldwater himself repeated, claimed his defense program consisted of ordering the drivers in his wagon train to form a circle.

In any event, Gold found evidence in the compartment containing the later editions of the paper that indicated Miss O'Connor might be the distributor. He went to her compartment but found she was eating an early breakfast in the dining car. Without her permission, he ordered her baggage searched and discovered further evidence proving conclusively she was the "spy." Gold then confronted Miss O'Connor. "This is your last delivery, dear," he told her.

He led her back to her compartment to pack, saying she would be put off the train in five minutes.

When Miss O'Connor discovered her luggage had been searched, she complained vociferously. The commotion brought a swarm of reporters rushing to the compartment. Miss O'Connor, with the reporters watching the remainder of the byplay, was forced to leave the train at Parkersburg, West Virginia. The resulting news stories made the Goldwater forces look worse than they would have if they had merely laughed off the spy in their midst. Only later did the Republicans learn they had suffered another indignity at the hands of Dick Tuck.

By 1968 Tuck had resumed making life miserable for Richard Nixon. Despite his losses in the 1960 presidential campaign and the 1962 gubernatorial race,

Nixon was favored to win the Republican presidential nomination at the 1968 national convention in Miami Beach. His campaign slogan—NIXON'S THE ONE—appeared on signs, campaign buttons, and other items distributed widely across the country. One of his major campaign planks called for cracking down on welfare cheaters. It was not a new theme for Nixon or some other candidates. For years, there had been claims that the ranks of welfare recipients were crowded with families in which unmarried women repeatedly gave birth to children, supposedly with the intention of collecting additional benefits. (Such benefits are partially based on the number of children in the household.) Although experts on the welfare system contended it was a spurious issue, Nixon continued to promise he would drive unwed mothers from the welfare rolls if elected president.

Although Nixon perhaps did not intend it that way, the issue took on racial connotations. Many voters assumed, wrongly, that welfare benefits were granted chiefly to poor blacks. Actually, many more whites than blacks were on the welfare rolls. In any event, there was an assumption in some quarters that Nixon meant he would drive unwed *black* mothers from the rolls.

Dick Tuck arranged a demonstration outside Nixon's Miami Beach hotel at the height of the Republican convention. A long line of women marched around the building. Each of the women was black and obviously pregnant. And each carried a picket sign that read, NIXON'S THE ONE!

Such stunts invariably made front-page news. Reporters liked Dick Tuck and thought his pranks livened

103

up what were often monotonous campaigns. Tuck began attracting imitators.

One campaigner who took a page from Tuck's book was John Lindsay. A former Republican congressman who became a Democrat after his election as mayor of New York, Lindsay sought the Democratic presidential nomination in 1972. In the Florida Democratic presidential primary, Lindsay faced his toughest competition from Alabama Governor George Wallace. Despite repeated challenges from Lindsay, Wallace refused to appear on the same platform with him and debate the issues.

One night when Wallace was scheduled to address a campaign dinner to which Lindsay had not been invited, the Lindsay organization sent undercover agents to infiltrate the banquet hall. The agents smuggled in eight chickens, all given anesthesia to prevent them from clucking and being prematurely discovered. When the chickens revived from the anesthesia, they were released and sent scurrying through the hall. Each wore a sign that read, I'M GEORGE WALLACE, AND I'M AFRAID TO DEBATE.

Invariably, candidates who feel they are leading in election campaigns are tempted to refuse to debate their opponents. "Why give the other guy publicity when I'm ahead?" such candidates argue. It has become one of the most tired tricks in the political book for a trailing candidate to debate "an empty chair" in such circumstances—claiming the front-runner is a coward. Lindsay's organization at least came up with an original way of making the point.

An even more ingenious technique for accomplishing

the same end was dreamed up by John F. (Jack) English, generally regarded as one of the shrewdest political strategists in the country. English learned politics at the knee of his mother, Anne, a long-time Democratic leader on Long Island. Mrs. English, who had been appointed a postmistress as a reward for her service to the party, sent her son on political errands from the time he was a small boy. By the time he was thirty-two, English had become Democratic county leader in Nassau County, Long Island—one of the youngest county leaders in the country. His county, however, had long been among the most determined Republican strongholds extant. Although there were almost two million people in the county, only about a third of the registered voters were Democrats. The Democrats had, in fact, never controlled the county government.

In 1961 English set out to reverse the trend. He presented voters with a new face—that of Eugene H. Nickerson—in the race for county executive (head of the county government). Nickerson, a descendant of John Adams, was a young, articulate lawyer who had impeccable credentials for public office. But he was virtually unknown among the voters. The Republicans nominated as his opponent an old-guard clubhouse politician named Robert Dill who was a poor speaker and seemed strangely unwise about the problems of suburban Nassau County. Often in speeches he seemed to make blunders that a candidate for president of a high school student council would know how to avoid.

Still, with Republicans outnumbering Democrats by such a wide margin, Dill seemed a relatively sure winner if he avoided mistakes. His advisers accordingly urged him to steer clear of debates with Nickerson, and Dill complied. At English's suggestion, Nickerson made Dill's refusal to debate a key issue in the campaign. English, from Democratic headquarters, issued a press release in which Nickerson complained: "Yesterday morning I spent two and a half hours talking to three different classes of students at a local high school. A similar invitation had been extended to my opponent . . . and turned down. . . ."

Long Island and New York City journalists, who had not been much impressed with Dill's performance, gave Nickerson's remarks extensive coverage. Still, Dill would not rise to the challenge. "I refuse to debate with Nickerson," he said. "I'm not furnishing an audience for him. He's on the bottom, and I'm going to keep him there."

English responded by offering to contribute $10,000 to Dill's campaign if the Republican would agree to debate Nickerson at any place of Dill's choosing. Once again, Dill refused. Finally, English carried the issue to an extreme guaranteed to receive even greater publicity for his candidate. He repeated the offer, if Dill would appear on television to debate the issues "with any eighth-grader in a Nassau school to be chosen by lot."

When an angry Dill still refused the challenge, the previously little-known Nickerson received yet more publicity. Finally, in the last week of the campaign, English further enraged Dill by accusing him of being less than honest in continuing to take part in a private brokerage business while serving in a federal job—U.S. customs collector in New York—by virtue of a patronage appointment. Dill, despite his advisers' restraining efforts, fell right into English's trap. He accused English, Nickerson, and their backers of conducting a "vicious" campaign, then told a Republican rally: "Let's give this gang of greasy, slimy pigs the beating of their life."

It was one thing to berate the opposition party. But it was quite another to call them and all their backers a "gang of greasy, slimy pigs." English, however, knew a political bonanza when he saw one.

The next day he rounded up bands of Democrats to picket Dill headquarters. All of them were wearing pig costumes and one was carrying a live pig. Dill became a laughing stock. Despite his clear advantage at the outset of the campaign, he lost the election to Nickerson— who went on to win national attention as one of the most effective county officials anywhere.

English was not always so successful at political fun and games as he had been in the 1961 Nickerson campaign. Only a year later, he found himself on the receiving end of one of the oldest political tricks.

The scene was the War Memorial Auditorium in Syracuse, where New York Democrats were conducting their state convention to choose a candidate to oppose Republican Governor Nelson Rockefeller's race for re-election. The Democratic mayor of New York City, Robert Wagner, favored federal prosecutor Robert Morgenthau for the nomination. Although Morgenthau had never before run for office and was little known outside New York City, Wagner had apparently accumulated enough support to ensure his nomination.

English, a rival of Wagner's for behind-the-scenes power in the statewide party, had his own candidate—

Queens County District Attorney Frank O'Connor. He had nothing against Morgenthau but felt O'Connor would run a stronger race and thus provide more help to other candidates on the Democratic ticket. English had been scurrying around the auditorium, trying to head off what seemed to be an effort to stampede the delegates into a hasty decision to nominate Morgenthau. He thought he was on the verge of stopping the Morgenthau bandwagon if only he could get the convention to recess until the following morning.

Seizing a microphone on the convention floor, English demanded to be recognized. The convention chairman, Albany Mayor Erastus Corning, who was considered a Morgenthau backer, ignored him.

"Mr. Chairman!" English shouted. But Corning, apparently wary of an attempted call for a recess, paid no attention. "Mr. Chairman! Mr. Chairman! Mr. Chairman!" English continued shouting.

Suddenly, his microphone went dead. Someone—presumably a Morgenthau supporter—had yanked the plug. As English well knew, politicians had been yanking microphone plugs from sockets since shortly after the discovery of electricity. But he was not about to let that stop him.

In a moment or two, the convention was treated to a riotous scene. English—still young and athletic—raced down an aisle, leaped over chairs and tables, and vaulted onto the convention platform. A stunned Chairman Corning found himself in a wrestling match with English for the main microphone. English was pulling back his right hand to throw a punch at Corning when a swarm of policemen and politicians swarmed all over him. When the tumult subsided, English did get his opportunity to ask for a recess—but Corning overruled him. Morgenthau was swiftly nominated, only to lose the election to Rockefeller by a wide margin.

English has masterminded numerous campaigns and was a close political adviser to both John F. Kennedy and Robert F. Kennedy. He continued to rise within the Democratic party ranks and was eventually chosen as counsel to the Democratic National Committee and chief political adviser in Senator Muskie's unsuccessful 1972 campaign for the Democratic presidential nomination. In both capacities, he found himself—along with other Democrats—on the receiving end of some of the dirty tricks involved in the Watergate affair.

Pranks and stunts have long been staples of American political life. Although new wrinkles turn up all the time, the basic elements have been around for years. The best stunts usually are remarkably simple.

Consider, for example, the act of political sabotage committed by Kentucky Republicans in 1928 against Democratic presidential candidate Al Smith. The Republicans, who supported Herbert Hoover's campaign against Smith, controlled the city government in Louisville. When they learned Smith planned to make a speech at a Louisville auditorium operated by the city, they decided to take advantage of the situation. Shortly before Smith's appearance, city maintenance workers were ordered to fire up the auditorium's boilers and operate the heating system at full blast, even though the weather was already uncomfortably warm.

By the time Smith began his speech the auditorium, packed with spectators, was steaming. And it kept get-

109

ting hotter. Journalist and author H. L. Mencken, who covered the speech, wrote:

> Before Al was halfway through his speech, he was sweating so copiously that he seemed half drowned. The dignitaries on the platform sweated, too, and so did the vulgar on the floor and in the galleries. Minute by minute the temperature seemed to increase until finally it became almost unbearable. When Al shut down at last, with his collar a rag and his shirt and pants sticking to his hide, the thermometer must have stood at 100 degrees at least, and there were plenty who would have guessed that it stood at 110.

James M. Curley—who served four times as Boston's mayor beginning in 1915 and also served two prison sentences on corruption charges—had a favorite trick that involved placing a classified advertisement in the Boston newspapers reading: "Late-model Cadillac, must sacrifice, excellent condition, $1,000." The phone number listed in the ad would be that of his opponent's campaign headquarters. Curley's trick served several purposes: it tied up his opponent's phone lines; it caused general confusion at the opponent's headquarters; and it created antagonism toward his opponent among the people who called, thinking a Cadillac was available.

Almost without exception, the tactics discussed in this chapter would be regarded by most political experts as within "the rules of the game" practiced in the United States. Perhaps some of them did little to enlighten the voters. Perhaps they did not elevate the political process. But, at least, they did not violate the law or grossly offend the public interest. To the extent that they enlivened campaigns and attracted voters' interest in the political process, they could be regarded (at least by some) as beneficial to the system by which office-holders were chosen.

9 NIXON'S DIRTY TRICKSTERS

Without question, the most notorious examples of dirty politics in the nation's history occurred during President Richard M. Nixon's 1972 re-election campaign. An astonishing array of illegal and unethical activities was carried out on Nixon's behalf.

How and why did all this happen?

One contributing element undoubtedly was the fact that Nixon was, in political terminology, "running scared." He was very much preoccupied with the close margins by which his previous two presidential campaigns had been decided. In his 1960 loss to John F. Kennedy, Nixon had trailed in the popular vote by only one-tenth of one percentage point. Then, in defeating Hubert H. Humphrey for the presidency in

1968, Nixon had led in the popular vote by just seven-tenths of a percentage point.

Moreover, despite Nixon's strong support of their campaigns, Republican candidates had fared poorly in the 1970 midterm elections. The Republicans had lost twelve seats in the House of Representatives and gained only two seats in the Senate—thus leaving both houses of Congress under the decisive control of the Democrats. At the same time, public opinion polls indicated deep currents of dissatisfaction with the Nixon administration among many voters.

Thus, as Nixon and his aides began planning for the 1972 presidential election, they had good reason to believe that his campaign might face serious difficulty. Against that background, they decided to go to extraordinary lengths to take every possible advantage of the Democrats. Normal standards of political morality were set aside in the zeal to win the election at any cost. Ambitious plans were prepared for spying on the Democrats, disrupting their campaign, and trying to sow dissension in the Democratic ranks through a broad range of dirty tricks.

Officials at the White House and at Nixon's campaign organization, the Committee for the Reelection of the President (CREEP), ordered the establishment of several secret teams assigned to carry out political espionage and harassment operations against the Democrats. Placed in charge of one such team was a young California lawyer named Donald H. Segretti. He was recruited for the job in June 1971 by Nixon's appointments secretary, Dwight Chapin.

Like several other White House aides, Chapin had

113

attended the University of Southern California (USC). Segretti had been one of his fellow students, and both had been active in campus politics. A particularly rough brand of dirty politics characterized by such tactics as stuffing of ballot boxes, sabotage of opponents' campaigns, and destruction of opponents' campaign literature was practiced on the USC campus. Chapin and Segretti had been deeply enmeshed in such activities. Thus it seemed natural for Chapin to tap Segretti when the decision was made to establish dirty-tricks operations for Nixon's re-election campaign.

Care was taken to cloak Segretti's activities in secrecy. Arrangements were made to have his salary and expenses paid from a secret fund of money left over from Nixon's 1968 presidential campaign. The fund was administered by the president's personal attorney, Herbert W. Kalmbach. On instructions from Chapin, Segretti used a series of assumed names—including Don Simmons, Don Morris, and Don Durham.

Under such names, Segretti began to travel around the country recruiting other young men and women to take part in the dirty-tricks operations. He drew the recruits from, among other sources, lists provided by Chapin of individuals who had worked in previous Nixon campaigns.

In Florida, for example, Segretti signed up as an aide a man named Robert M. Benz, who had formerly headed a Young Republican organization. With the help of an assistant named Douglas Kelly, Benz hired seven others to take part in the spying and sabotage operations. One of them, a secretary, obtained a job in the Florida primary campaign headquarters of Senator

114

Edmund Muskie of Maine—then regarded as the front-runner for the Democratic presidential nomination. Another got a similar job in the headquarters of Senator Henry Jackson of Washington state, also a Democratic presidential contender. Both women secretly provided Segretti with confidential memoranda, scheduling information, lists of financial contributors, and other material filched from the Democrats' files.

Meanwhile, Segretti's other recruits were pulling a series of tricks designed to disrupt the Democratic candidates' campaigns. They set off at least four stink bombs aimed at harassing Senator Muskie's operations —two at his Florida headquarters and two at campaign picnics crowded with voters. Once, Douglas Kelly sneaked into a Muskie news conference and released two white mice whose tails were bedecked with ribbons reading, MUSKIE IS A RAT FINK. He also turned loose a small bird. The resulting disturbance turned the press conference into a shambles. On another occasion, Kelly hired a young woman to run naked outside Muskie's hotel room while shouting, "I love Ed Muskie."

During the campaign, Muskie had come out in favor of busing to promote school desegregation—a highly unpopular policy in Florida. To capitalize on the issue, Segretti distributed several hundred posters reading, HELP MUSKIE IN BUSING MORE CHILDREN NOW. The posters were ostensibly signed by an organization calling itself the Mothers Backing Muskie Committee. But the committee was nonexistent; it was a figment of Segretti's fertile imagination.

Segretti and his subordinates made repeated efforts to create antagonism among the Democratic presidential

115

candidates. At a Florida rally for Democratic contender Governor George Wallace of Alabama, they distributed more than 1,000 anti-Wallace cards that purported to come from the Muskie camp. On one side, the cards read, IF YOU LIKED HITLER, YOU'LL JUST LOVE WALLACE. On the other side, they read, CAST YOUR VOTE FOR SENATOR EDMUND MUSKIE. Actually, the Muskie organization had nothing to do with the cards; they had been printed on Segretti's orders. But Wallace staff members, who had no way of knowing that, naturally became embittered against Muskie and his campaigners. In a similar operation outside Miami Beach synagogues, Segretti's underlings distributed leaflets assailing Muskie's position on U.S. policy toward Israel. The leaflets bore legends falsely claiming they had been issued by another Democratic contender, New York Mayor John V. Lindsay.

Perhaps the most vicious trick pulled by Segretti in Florida was the mailing of a scurrilous letter falsely accusing two of the Democratic presidential candidates of sexual and other improprieties. With the help of his spy in the Muskie organization, Segretti obtained some Muskie campaign stationery. He sent the stationery, along with a typewritten copy of the scurrilous letter, to Robert Benz. One of Benz's subordinates then had the letter reproduced on the stationery, and three days before the Florida primary it was mailed to voters identified as backers of Senator Jackson.

"We on the Sen. Ed Muskie staff sincerely hope that you have decided upon Senator Muskie as your choice," the letter said. "However, if you have not made your decision, you should be aware of several facts." It then

116

went on to charge that Senator Jackson had fathered an illegitimate child by a seventeen-year-old girl while a high school student in 1929. It also claimed that Jackson had been arrested on homosexual charges in Washington, D.C., in 1955 and 1957. Further, it accused another Democratic presidential contender, Senator Hubert H. Humphrey, of having been arrested on drunk-driving charges in Washington in 1967 while having a "well-known call girl" in his car. As Segretti later admitted, there was no truth to any of these allegations; he had simply made them up.

When Segretti reported to White House aide Dwight Chapin on the letter's distribution, Chapin congratulated him on his ingenuity. He said Chapin told him that, although the operation had cost only about $20, it had been worth between $10,000 and $20,000 to the Nixon campaign. Douglas Kelly said later that such tactics were designed not so much to influence votes as to create dissension among the Democratic contenders and thus make it more difficult for them to unite behind one candidate for the eventual campaign against Nixon. "The idea was to get the [Democratic] candidates backbiting each other and possibly starting doing it to each other outside of our activities," Kelly said.

In any event, Senator Muskie—the main target of Segretti's Florida activities—ran a poor race in that state's primary: he finished third. Governor Wallace won the primary, with Senator Humphrey finishing second.

Nonetheless, Muskie was still regarded as the Democratic front-runner at that point—so Segretti continued to concentrate on harassing him in the next important

117

primary, in Wisconsin. Robert Benz traveled to Wisconsin with Segretti, and they distributed literature and bumper strips with disparaging sexual remarks about Muskie. They also created confusion in his campaign organization by ordering a steady stream of unwanted items—such as large quantities of pizza, fried chicken, and floral arrangements—sent to Muskie's hotel. In addition, they ordered undesired limousine service for Muskie. The orders were placed in the name of a Muskie staff member and were billed to the Muskie campaign organization.

Segretti and Benz also found time to pull at least one dirty trick on Senator Humphrey in Wisconsin. Throughout Milwaukee's black neighborhoods, they distributed phony invitations to a free lunch with Humphrey. The invitations promised "all you can eat," plus beer, wine, and soda. They also promised that Mrs. Martin Luther King and actor Lorne Greene would be present, along with Humphrey. The supposed lunch was nonexistent. When residents turned out, they found neither food nor drink nor Humphrey nor Greene nor Mrs. King. Needless to say, they went away disgruntled.

The Wisconsin Democratic primary was won by Senator George McGovern of South Dakota. Governor Wallace finished second, Senator Humphrey third, and Senator Muskie a poor fourth. Still, Segretti continued his harassment campaign against Muskie.

In advance of the Democratic primary in the District of Columbia, Muskie's organization had scheduled a fund-raising dinner to be attended by about 1,300 guests at the Washington Hilton Hotel. Segretti, with the help of Douglas Kelly, set about disrupting the dinner. They saw to it that the hotel was inundated with unwanted deliveries, all billed to the Muskie campaign dinner. Posing as members of the Muskie organization, they arranged for two magicians to show up at the hotel, expecting to entertain the guests. Organizers of the dinner, who knew nothing about the magicians, refused to permit them to perform. A great commotion ensued, during which one of the magicians told the organizers, "If you don't let us in, we'll turn you into something terrible."

Further confusion was created because Segretti and Kelly had issued phony dinner invitations to numerous foreign ambassadors stationed in Washington. Sixteen ambassadors showed up in limousines ordered by Segretti and Kelly (and billed to the Muskie campaign). Their arrival created embarrassment on several grounds. For one thing, a detailed seating plan had been worked out for the dinner and there were initially no seats for the ambassadors. But rather than touch off a potential international incident, the dinner organizers juggled their plans and found places for the unexpected dignitaries. For another thing, such a political fund-raising dinner was an inappropriate occasion for attendance by foreign diplomats. Traditionally, foreigners have been expected to keep their distance from internal American political activities. Once the ambassadors had arrived, however, the dinner organizers had little choice except to welcome them.

While Segretti was pulling such tricks, his subordinates continued their divisive efforts elsewhere. When the various Democratic contenders made public appear-

119

ances throughout the country, they were frequently confronted by demonstrators carrying picket signs denouncing them and supporting one of their rivals for the presidential nomination. The demonstrators pretended to represent the rival Democratic candidates but actually were part of Segretti's organization. Candidates being picketed, however, had no way of knowing that. They assumed their competitors were trying to disrupt their campaigns. As a result, just as Segretti had planned, additional resentment developed among the Democratic contenders.

At the same time, unknown to Segretti, several other operations aimed at spying on and harassing the Democratic candidates were being conducted under the direction of the White House and President Nixon's reelection committee. One such operation was supervised by Jeb Stuart Magruder, a former special assistant to Nixon at the White House who had become deputy campaign director of CREEP.

Magruder approached Ken Rietz, youth director for CREEP, about helping plant a spy in Senator Muskie's Washington campaign headquarters. Rietz, in turn, passed the request to a friend named John Buckley, a former private detective serving as director of the inspection division of the U.S. Office of Economic Opportunity. At Buckley's instigation, a taxi driver named Elmer Wyatt volunteered his services to the Muskie headquarters. Magruder arranged for the Nixon campaign to pay Wyatt $1,000 a month for spying on the Muskie organization.

Initially, Muskie's staffers assigned Wyatt only to run routine errands in his cab. But in time he was en-

120

trusted to deliver confidential campaign papers between Muskie's political headquarters and his Senate office. When instructed to make such deliveries, Wyatt telephoned Buckley and set up appointments to meet him on a Washington street. Then, while Wyatt drove him around the downtown area in the cab, Buckley photographed the Muskie documents. This arrangement eventually became inconvenient, so Buckley rented a downtown office in which to do the photographing. Among the papers he copied were Muskie's proposed position papers on issues, memos on political strategy, advance texts of speeches, and schedules for planned campaign trips.

After getting the films developed, Buckley delivered them to Rietz, who relayed them to Magruder. Copies of important items culled from the Muskie documents were sent to the White House by Magruder's office. Information from the documents proved invaluable to Nixon campaign officials. Advance information on where Muskie would be making campaign appearances, for example, enabled the Nixon staffers to arrange for demonstrators to harass the Democratic contender. Similarly, advance knowledge of the positions Muskie would be taking on controversial issues allowed the Nixon organization time to develop strategy for undercutting his statements. In several cases, Nixon campaign officials leaked to friendly newspaper columnists portions of Muskie's internal staff memos that could be used to embarrass him. The contents of one such memo were twisted in such a fashion as to lead to publication of a column charging that Muskie was enlisting the help of foreign policy advisers who held extreme left-wing views.

Magruder also supervised another operation aimed at harassing Muskie's campaign. He instructed Herbert Porter, a former White House aide who had become scheduling director for CREEP, to find someone to travel to the presidential primary states and seek ways of embarrassing Muskie. A young Californian named Roger Greaves was hired for the job.

Greaves saw to it that pickets—many of them dressed in hippie fashion—demonstrated against Muskie while posing as supporters of other Democratic candidates. During the New Hampshire primary campaign, Porter said, Greaves arranged for voters to get annoying late-night telephone calls from persons identifying themselves as members of a supposed Harlem for Muskie Committee. The callers promised that Muskie would work to obtain "full justice for black people." Since New Hampshire had few black residents and advancement of blacks' rights was scarcely a popular issue in the state, most of the calls received antagonistic responses. Other New Hampshire residents received repeated late-night calls from persons who identified themselves as Muskie supporters and asked again and again for identical information on election issues. Muskie campaign workers said such tactics caused many voters to become infuriated at the Maine senator.

Greaves ultimately quit working for CREEP, and his job was taken over by a private detective named Michael McMinoway from Louisville, Kentucky. In addition to harassing Muskie, McMinoway infiltrated the organizations of Senators Humphrey and McGovern

122

during the California primary campaign. He sent secret memos to CREEP on confidential information picked up at McGovern and Humphrey campaign offices.

Another political spying operation by the Nixon forces was supervised by E. Howard Hunt, a former Central Intelligence Agency (CIA) agent who had been hired as a White House consultant and would ultimately become a central figure in the Watergate scandal. Hunt hired Thomas J. Gregory, a history major at Brigham Young University in Utah, and instructed him to try to infiltrate Muskie's Washington headquarters. Gregory received permission from university administrators to obtain college credits for supposed off-campus studies in Washington. He then went to Muskie's headquarters, where he volunteered to work in the campaign. His offer was accepted, and he was assigned to duties in the campaign's foreign affairs section. Gregory prepared written reports for Hunt on documents crossing his desk and discussions of Muskie campaign strategy. Once a week, he met Hunt at a downtown Washington drugstore and delivered the reports. When Muskie's campaign later faltered, Gregory easily switched his operation to Senator McGovern's headquarters and continued feeding reports to Hunt.

Still another political intelligence mission was directed by Murray Chotiner, a long-time political adviser to President Nixon. Chotiner paid two free-lance writers, Seymour K. Freidin and Lucianne Goldberg, to pose as journalists covering the Democratic contenders and send him reports on information that could help the Nixon campaign. Freidin concentrated on the Muskie campaign but also traveled with several other

123

Democratic candidates. Miss Goldberg spied on the McGovern campaign. She said later she was instructed to look for "really dirty stuff" such as "who was sleeping with whom . . . who was smoking pot on the [campaign] plane—that sort of thing."

One of the most celebrated dirty tricks of the campaign was pulled about two weeks before the New Hampshire primary. A fraudulent letter signed with a fake name and address ("Paul Morrison of Deerfield Beach, Florida") was published in the Manchester, New Hampshire, *Union Leader*—an arch-conservative newspaper that strongly opposed Senator Muskie's candidacy. The letter claimed Muskie had been asked, while campaigning in Florida, what he knew about black people. "He didn't have any in Maine, a man with the senator said," the letter asserted. "No blacks, but we have 'Canucks.' What did he mean? We asked— Mr. Muskie laughed and said come to New England and see."

"Canuck" is the derogatory name for people of French-Canadian background, and both Maine and New Hampshire have large concentrations of residents of French-Canadian descent. The *Union Leader*, in addition to publishing the letter, carried a front-page editorial accusing Muskie of insulting them. The following day, the newspaper reprinted a magazine article that painted an unflattering picture of Muskie's wife, Jane. Among other things, the article claimed Mrs. Muskie had invited reporters to join her in telling "dirty jokes" and had told them she liked "two drinks before dinner and a crème de menthe afterward."

Two days after publication of the so-called Canuck

letter, Muskie made an emotional response. He stood on a flatbed truck outside the office of the *Union Leader* and attacked the newspaper's controversial publisher, William Loeb, as a "gutless coward." Muskie emphatically denied he or anyone associated with his campaign had made any such statements as those mentioned in the Canuck letter. Then, referring to the uncomplimentary published references to his wife, he broke down and cried.

His loss of composure did severe damage to his campaign. Muskie had been trying throughout the campaign to project the image of a calm, unruffled political leader who would make decisions on a rational rather than emotional basis. The crying episode, which received wide coverage in the news media, put a sharp dent in that image. Muskie's political opponents exploited the incident at every opportunity. Publisher Loeb claimed it demonstrated that Muskie was "not the man that many of us want to have his finger on the nuclear button." In the New Hampshire primary, where Muskie had initially been expected to win decisively, he made a far poorer showing than anticipated.

Although the precise authorship of the Canuck letter has never been officially determined, there is little doubt that it was part of the Nixon campaign's dirty-tricks operations. Both journalists and government investigators scoured the vicinity of Deerfield Beach, Florida, but could never find any trace of a man named Paul Morrison. *Washington Post* reporter Marilyn Berger said Kenneth Clawson, deputy communications director at the Nixon White House, told her he had written the letter. When she pressed him for an explanation, Clawson told her, "Muskie was the candidate who would represent the strongest opposition and they [Clawson's superiors] wanted him out." Clawson denied making such statements or writing the letter. But even if he did not write it, there is general agreement that someone connected with the Nixon campaign did.

The examples of dirty politics discussed in this chapter were themselves serious breaches of campaign ethics. But in retrospect, they seem to represent preludes to the single most flagrant episode in the 1972 presidential campaign: the Watergate affair.

PART THREE

THE WATERGATE SCANDAL

10 BURGLARS AND "BUGS"

In addition to the piecemeal spying and dirty-tricks operations conducted on President Richard Nixon's behalf in the 1972 race, his campaign organization decided to establish an overall political-intelligence-gathering system. Assigned to draw up a broad-scale plan and supervise its activities was a flamboyant character named G. Gordon Liddy, who was appointed as general legal counsel to CREEP on November 24, 1971.

Controversy had pursued Liddy throughout his career—a circumstance that seemed to delight him. He had been an FBI agent in the early 1960s but had reportedly been persuaded by his superiors to resign because of his penchant for firing a gun when it was not necessary. Later, he became an assistant district attorney in Dutchess County, New York, and continued

129

to demonstrate his fondness for guns. Although his prosecutor's job gave him no police powers, he constantly toted a pistol in a shoulder holster. Once, while arguing a case before a jury, he suddenly whipped a gun from his pocket and fired a shot into the courtroom ceiling.

After running unsuccessfully for Congress in 1968, Liddy landed a job in the Nixon administration as a special assistant to the treasury secretary in charge of combating organized crime. He was forced out of that job, however, when he publicly lobbied against the administration's proposals for gun-control legislation. Nonetheless, he was soon given another assignment by the Nixon forces. He was hired as a member of the White House special investigations unit—better known as the Plumbers—a covert group assigned to plug embarrassing leaks of administration secrets and harass persons designated as political enemies of Nixon. Later investigations would reveal that the Plumbers had used such means as burglaries and illegal wiretaps in carrying out their questionable mission.

Although Liddy provided the re-election committee with legal advice on election and campaign finance laws and other matters, he spent most of his time on the duties he liked best—as head of CREEP's intelligence operation. In preliminary discussions of the intelligence program with Jeb Magruder, deputy campaign director of CREEP, Liddy said White House officials had promised him a $1 million budget for the project. Magruder told him that any program with a budget that large would need the approval of Attorney General John Mitchell, Nixon's former law partner, who would soon leave his government job to become head of CREEP. Liddy was instructed by Magruder to draw up detailed plans that could be presented to Mitchell for his approval.

On January 27, 1972, Liddy was ushered into Mitchell's private office at the Justice Department to make a "sales pitch" for his program. Present with Mitchell to hear the presentation were Magruder and John Dean, the White House legal counsel to President Nixon. Liddy brought with him six large, elaborate color charts detailing various sections of his plan. Each section was given a code designation using the name of a precious stone, such as "Ruby" or "Diamond," and the entire scheme was code-named "Project Gemstone." Referring periodically to the charts, Liddy proposed a wide array of political spying activities and dirty tricks to be used during the campaign.

Among his proposals were:

1. Planting wiretaps and electronic bugging devices in the Democratic National Committee offices at the Watergate office building in Washington, in the hotel rooms of prominent politicians attending the Democratic National Convention in Miami Beach, and in the campaign headquarters of the presidential candidate ultimately chosen by the Democrats. Liddy even envisioned using a so-called chase plane to intercept radio-telephone conversations between the Democratic candidate's campaign aircraft and his aides on the ground.

2. Committing burglaries at Democratic offices to obtain photographic copies of secret campaign documents.

3. Hiring prostitutes to lure prominent Democrats

131

into compromising situations in both Washington and Miami Beach. Liddy suggested renting a large yacht at Miami Beach during the Democratic convention and fitting it out with hidden cameras and tape recorders that would be used to gather evidence of improprieties by politicians enticed aboard the vessel by the prostitutes. The films and recordings would then be used to blackmail the politicians.

4. Kidnaping the leaders of radical groups that planned demonstrations against Nixon at the Republican National Convention. Liddy's plan called for drugging the radical leaders and holding them captive at secret locations in Mexico until the Republican convention ended. He pledged that the radicals would never learn who had kidnaped them or where they had been held.

5. Using teams of hired toughs to beat up protesters who staged demonstrations against Nixon at the Republican convention.

Despite the blatant illegality and bizarre nature of Liddy's various schemes, nobody at the meeting reprimanded him for coming up with such outlandish plans and presenting them in the office of the nation's highest law enforcement official. Dean later said he found the proposals "mind-boggling" and that Mitchell was "amazed" by them. Magruder described himself as "appalled" by the plans. Still, Mitchell told Liddy merely that the proposals were "not quite" what he had in mind. He said the $1 million budget was far too high, suggesting that Liddy "go back to the drawing boards and come up with a more realistic plan."

When the meeting broke up, Liddy was visibly disturbed by the rejection of his plan. Magruder told him to cheer up. "You just tone the plan down a little and we'll try again," Magruder said.

Liddy grudgingly went "back to the drawing boards" and prepared a less grandiose plan calling for a budget of $500,000. He abandoned the proposals for kidnapings, beating up anti-Nixon demonstrators, using a chase plane, and employing prostitutes aboard a yacht off Miami Beach. For the most part, Liddy's new scheme concentrated on using wiretaps, electronic bugs, and burglaries to obtain Democratic campaign secrets.

On February 4 Liddy returned to Mitchell's Justice Department office with Magruder and Dean to review the revised plan. Mitchell complained that the $500,000 budget was still too high and that further cuts were required. Dean protested that it was inappropriate to discuss such matters as illegal burglaries and electronic eavesdropping in the office of the attorney general of the United States. The meeting disbanded a short time later with a frustrated Liddy resigned to making additional reductions in his plan.

During the next several weeks, Liddy refined his proposal. It called for an initial burglary at the Democratic headquarters in the Watergate complex, during which a wiretap would be placed on Democratic National Chairman Lawrence O'Brien's telephone. Later, if funds were available, additional targets would be chosen. Liddy prepared and delivered to Magruder a detailed written plan for this third version of the project —including estimates on how many persons he would have to hire and how much equipment he would need. The revised budget, under this plan, came to $250,000.

When he received no quick response to the new proposal, Liddy began pressing for a decision. He went to the White House to see Charles Colson, a special counsel to the president regarded by many as a Nixon "hatchet man." Liddy complained that he had thus far been unable to win approval for his intelligence plan. Colson immediately telephoned Magruder. "Why don't you guys get off the stick and get Liddy's budget approved?" he asked. "We need the information, particularly on O'Brien." Magruder replied that the proposal was still under consideration. "We'll get to it as fast as we can," he said.

At the time, Magruder was also under pressure from elsewhere in the White House to get the plan approved. Gordon Strachan, assistant to Nixon's chief aide, H. R. Haldeman, called Magruder with instructions from Haldeman to "get this going." Strachan added, "The President wants it done, and there's to be no more arguing about it."

Near the end of March, by which time he had resigned as attorney general and officially taken over as head of CREEP, John Mitchell went on a brief vacation at Key Biscayne, Florida. On March 30, Magruder visited him there to discuss several dozen matters awaiting decision concerning the Nixon re-election campaign. Among them was the Liddy project. Magruder presented Mitchell with Liddy's revised written plan. He would later say Mitchell approved the plan at that time, telling him, "Okay, let's give him [Liddy] a quarter of a million dollars and let's see what he can come up with." Mitchell would later deny ever giving final approval to the plan. But in view of what happened after the Key

Biscayne meeting, most investigators of the affair have tended to believe Magruder's account.

Upon his return to Washington, Magruder notified Liddy that the plan had been approved and Liddy began putting the project into operation. He enlisted as his chief aide E. Howard Hunt, the former CIA agent and White House consultant who had also been involved in some of the Nixon campaign's dirty-tricks escapades. Hunt had worked with Liddy as a member of the White House Plumbers unit. Another early recruit was James W. McCord, Jr., a former FBI and CIA agent who had become chief of security for CREEP. An expert on electronic eavesdropping, McCord was placed in charge of wiretapping and bugging operations for the Liddy project.

Hunt, while in the CIA, had helped direct the 1961 Bay of Pigs operation, in which a force of Cuban exiles organized by the intelligence agency had invaded Cuba and made an unsuccessful attempt to overthrow the government of Premier Fidel Castro. Many of the Cuban exiles involved in the invasion, who now lived in the Miami area, had stayed in touch with Hunt over the years and remained intensely loyal to him. He had used some of them to commit a burglary on behalf of the Plumbers. Now, he recruited four of them—Bernard Barker, Frank Sturgis, Eugenio Martinez, and Virgilio Gonzalez—to take part in Liddy's project.

Liddy informed Hunt and McCord in mid-April that the Democratic National Committee headquarters in the Watergate would be their first target. He gave Mc-Cord $65,000 and instructed him to buy the electronic equipment needed for the operation. To avoid the suspicion that might result if he made unusually large purchases in any one place, McCord bought the equipment from a wide variety of suppliers in Chicago, Washington, and New York. Among the items he obtained were tiny eavesdropping devices, transmitters, walkie-talkies, antennas, and tape recorders.

Hunt flew to Miami and briefed the Cuban exiles on the Watergate burglary plan. Virgilio Gonzalez, a locksmith, would be expected to pick any locks necessary to gain entry to the Democratic National Committee office. Eugenio Martinez would be in charge of photographing confidential Democratic documents the burglars hoped to find. Bernard Barker would choose the documents to be photographed. Frank Sturgis would serve as a lookout and provide any help needed by the other men.

The building in which the Democratic National Committee office was situated was one of six in the luxurious Watergate complex overlooking the Potomac River. The complex included a second office building, a hotel, and three cooperative apartment buildings. In preparation for the burglary, Hunt and McCord made two visits to the target area to study the location of exits and entrances, staircases, elevators, and other means of access.

Across the street from the Watergate was a Howard Johnson's Motor Lodge. McCord rented a room there that provided a clear view of the Democratic National Committee office, for use both as a lookout post during the burglary and as a spot from which to monitor the wiretapping devices he planned to install. To man this post McCord recruited a former FBI agent, Alfred C. Baldwin, who had been doing security work for CREEP.

Liddy decided the burglary should take place over the Memorial Day weekend. Since a guard would be on duty at the office building, the burglars needed a means of getting past him to the building's interior. Hunt came up with the idea of renting the Continental Room, a banquet and conference room in the office building, on the pretext that he and the Cuban exiles were businessmen planning a dinner meeting. The Continental Room provided access to a corridor and stairway leading to the building's sixth floor, where the Democratic office was situated. Hunt arranged to reserve the banquet room for the night of Friday, May 26.

Barker, Gonzalez, Martinez, and Sturgis flew from Miami to Washington on May 22 and divided their time in the next few days between briefings on the planned burglary and sight-seeing tours. They checked into the Watergate Hotel, using false names, on the afternoon of May 26. Hunt also took a room at the hotel. Meanwhile, he rented a motion-picture projector and a travel film from a camera shop and put them in place before a movie screen in the Continental Room—hoping to add authenticity to the claim that he and his associates planned an actual business meeting there.

About 8 P.M., Hunt and his companions gathered in the Continental Room. They were served a sumptuous dinner catered by employees of the Watergate Hotel. After finishing the meal, they told their waiter they did not want to be disturbed for the rest of the night because the business portion of their meeting was about to begin. Hunt turned on the motion-picture projector and began showing the travel film to allay the suspicions of anyone passing outside the room. Shortly after mid-

137

night, Gonzalez took his tools from a briefcase and began trying to pick the lock on the door leading from the Continental Room to the corridor providing access to other floors of the building. Although he worked feverishly, he was unable to get the door opened. Hunt reluctantly ordered the operation scrubbed for the night.

But the following evening another attempt was made by different means to enter the Democratic office. McCord and the Cuban exiles, again pretending to be businessmen, walked into the lobby of the office building. They told the guard they were visiting the Federal Reserve Board office on the eighth floor and signed false names in the visitors' log. After riding the elevator to the eighth floor, they walked down two flights of stairs to the Democratic office. When Gonzalez tried picking the lock on the office door, however, he again encountered trouble. He complained that the lock was an old-fashioned model and that he did not have the tools necessary to open it. Barker radioed word of the problem by walkie-talkie to Hunt and Liddy, who were waiting in Hunt's Watergate Hotel room, and they ordered the operation aborted again.

After the burglary team returned from the office building, Hunt instructed Gonzalez to fly to Miami to get the additional tools he needed. Gonzalez made a quick round trip, arriving back in Washington late the following afternoon. That night, the team made a third attempt. Gonzalez and Sturgis walked into the office building's underground garage, and Gonzalez succeeded in picking the lock on a door leading to a staircase. The two men placed a strip of tape across the door latch, which held the door slightly ajar so that other members of the team could follow them later. They walked up to the sixth floor, where Gonzalez went to work on the door to the Democratic office with the new tools he had brought from Miami. This time, he was able to pry open the lock.

Once inside the office, Gonzalez and Sturgis radioed word of their success to Hunt and Liddy at the Watergate Hotel. Hunt instructed McCord, Barker, and Martinez to join the other two burglars. Following the same route taken by Gonzalez and Sturgis, the trio soon arrived at the Democratic headquarters.

McCord immediately set to work planting his wiretaps. First, he placed one on a "call director"—a device controlling several telephone extensions used by Democratic National Chairman O'Brien. Next, for insurance, he put a second tap on a phone in an adjoining room used by R. Spencer Oliver, executive director of the Association of State Democratic Chairmen. Using a portable testing instrument, McCord checked both taps and found them in working order.

While McCord worked on the taps, Barker searched file cabinets and desks for confidential documents. He selected about three dozen documents, including security plans for the Democratic National Convention and papers relating to campaign operations and financial contributions. Martinez photographed the documents, and they were then returned to the places where Barker had found them. When the burglars finished their work, they went back to Hunt's hotel room, where Liddy congratulated them on "a good job."

After catching a few hours of sleep, McCord met Alfred Baldwin in the listening-post room on the fourth floor of the Howard Johnson's Motor Lodge to start monitoring the wiretaps. The wiretapping devices Mc-Cord had planted were actually miniature radio transmitters equipped with low-strength power supplies to prevent detection by outsiders. Using a sophisticated receiving device, McCord succeeded in pulling in signals from the tap on R. Spencer Oliver's telephone. He was unable, however, to pick up signals from the tap on the call director controlling O'Brien's extensions. McCord fiddled incessantly with the receiver dials and tried using a substitute antenna but still had no success. Thinking he might have better luck from a point higher in the building, McCord moved to a room on the seventh floor. Still, he could locate no signals from the O'Brien tap. He ultimately quit searching, assuming that something had gone wrong with the wiretap device or that there was too much metal shielding in the walls around O'Brien's office to permit the signals to reach the listening post.

There seemed no choice, at least temporarily, except to be content with monitoring the conversations on Oliver's phone. Every business day, during the normal working hours at the Democratic headquarters, Baldwin sat before a monitoring unit in the listening-post room. The unit contained a small screen resembling those on television sets. When nobody was talking on Oliver's phone, a steady line would run across the screen. But when the phone was in use, the line would become scrambled. Baldwin would immediately put on a set of earphones and begin transcribing the conversation.

McCord reviewed the transcripts and, when he found something of political importance, wrote a report summarizing the conversation and quoting from Baldwin's logs. He delivered the reports and transcripts to Liddy. Liddy, in turn, instructed his secretary to retype portions of the transcripts on stationery bearing the letterhead "Gemstone."

Bernard Barker took the film of the documents photographed at the Democratic headquarters to a Miami camera shop for processing. The shop's owner, Michael Richardson, developed and printed thirty-eight glossy pictures from the film on a rush basis. They showed the documents being held in gloved hands. Some of them bore the heading "Chairman, Democratic National Committee." When handing the pictures to Barker, Richardson said, "It's real cloak-and-dagger stuff, isn't it?" Barker nodded his head in agreement but said nothing. E. Howard Hunt flew to Miami, picked up the pictures from Barker, then returned immediately to Washington and gave them to Liddy.

Liddy delivered the pictures and periodic summaries of the wiretapped conversations to Jeb Magruder, the deputy campaign director of CREEP. Magruder and other officials involved in the Nixon re-election campaign were disappointed that the materials did not contain more useful information.

Magruder says he showed the photographs and wiretap summaries to White House aide Gordon Strachan, who complained that Liddy was "just wasting our time and money." Strachan, however, denies ever seeing the documents or making such a comment.

Magruder says he also showed the materials to John Mitchell. By Magruder's account, which is heatedly denied by Mitchell, the former attorney general examined the photographs and wiretap summaries, then ordered Liddy into his office. Magruder says Mitchell angrily told Liddy, "This stuff isn't worth the paper it's printed on." Liddy explained that McCord had been unable to pick up signals from the wiretap placed on O'Brien's telephone extensions. He promised to get the situation corrected and produce satisfactory results.

In any event, it was decided to order the burglary team to break into the Democrats' Watergate office a second time. Additional documents were to be photographed and attempts were to be made to solve the problem of the ineffective wiretap on O'Brien's phone extensions. McCord was also to plant a room bug in O'Brien's office—that is, a device that would pick up discussions within the room, rather than telephone conversations.

Meanwhile, members of the team had made several attempts to burglarize and wiretap the Washington headquarters of Senator George McGovern, who by that time had emerged as the leading contender for the Democratic presidential nomination. But, each time, they had been forced to abandon the mission because McGovern campaign volunteers were working late into the night at the headquarters. Now, it was decided that, after committing the planned second burglary at the Watergate, they would take another crack at McGovern headquarters.

Hunt, Liddy, McCord, Barker, Gonzalez, Sturgis, and Martinez met in a room at the Watergate Hotel early on the evening of June 16. They discussed plans for making their second entry into the Democratic National Committee office later that night. Hunt gave each of the five burglars two $100 bills for use as potential bribe money in the event they were captured. He took their billfolds, containing their legal identification papers, for safekeeping. McCord and Sturgis were given false identification papers; the three other burglars already had phony papers used on past escapades.

Shortly before 10 P.M., McCord walked to the Watergate office building lobby and rode the elevator to the eighth floor. He then walked down the stairs to the underground garage, placing strips of tape across the latches of a series of doors on various floors so that the doors could be opened from either side. On the garage level, he taped the latches of three doors providing access to the staircase. When he had finished, he returned to the Watergate Hotel room and reported to Liddy and Hunt. He then crossed the street to the listening-post room at the Howard Johnson's Motor Lodge, where Alfred Baldwin was stationed as a lookout.

From the listening post, McCord and Baldwin could see that lights were still burning in the Democratic office and that one man was still working there. The man was Bruce Givner, a Columbia University student working for the Democrats as a summer intern. McCord reported the situation to Hunt by telephone, and they and their associates settled down to await Givner's departure from the office.

Shortly after midnight, a private security guard named Frank Wills began making a routine tour of the office building. Wills discovered a strip of tape across the latch of one of the doors on the garage level. He removed the tape but did not consider it important at

143

the time—assuming that it had been placed there by a member of the building's maintenance staff.

About 12:45 A.M., Bruce Givner finally turned off the lights and left the office. McCord notified Hunt that the coast appeared clear, then walked across to the Watergate Hotel room to join the other members of the burglary team. Before leaving the Howard Johnson's, he cautioned Baldwin to keep a sharp eye on the street and the Watergate and to report any unusual activity by walkie-talkie.

A few minutes after McCord's arrival at the Watergate Hotel, he and the four other burglars left for the office-building garage. When they arrived, they were shocked to find that the tape had been removed from the latch and that the door leading to the staircase was locked. Leaving Gonzalez to try picking the lock, the others trooped back to the hotel room to discuss with Hunt and Liddy whether to proceed with the burglary or call it off for the night. While the discussion was in progress, Gonzalez reported by walkie-talkie that he had unlocked the garage-level door. It was decided to proceed with the operation.

Gonzalez retaped the door latch and walked up the stairs to the sixth floor, where he was soon joined by the others. But when he attempted to pick the lock on the door to the Democratic office, he again encountered trouble. The lock, old and rusty, would not budge. Compounding the problem was the fact that the door did not fit properly into its frame. After Gonzalez had worked on the lock for more than a half hour without success, the burglars decided to try a new tack. They would take off the entire door. After knocking pins out

144

of the hinges, they lifted the door away from the frame, entered the office, then hung the door back in place.

Barker radioed Hunt to report that they were inside the office. Barker then began searching the files for documents to be photographed. Others started removing panels from the ceiling of O'Brien's office so that Mc-Cord could plant a room "bug" there.

Meanwhile, security guard Frank Wills was making another tour of the office building. When he reached the garage level, he was taken aback to discover that a new strip of tape had been placed across the latch of the door leading to the staircase. Realizing that something was obviously amiss, Wills called the police at about 1:50 A.M.

A dispatcher for the Washington Metropolitan Police Department issued a radio call, asking whether any patrol car from the department's Tactical Squadron was in the area. Sergeant Paul Leeper and Officers John Barrett and Carl Shoffler, members of a special Tactical Squadron unit assigned to dress in casual clothes and ride unmarked cars, replied that their car was only a couple of minutes away from the Watergate. The dispatcher ordered them to drive to the office building and meet Wills.

Alfred Baldwin, manning his lookout post on the balcony outside the room at the Howard Johnson's, watched as the car pulled up to the office building and the three men walked inside. But since the car was unmarked and the men were not wearing police uniforms, he placed no immediate importance on their arrival. Inside the building, Wills showed the officers the taped door latch and told them that there had been several

145

recent attempted burglaries on the sixth and eighth floors. The officers instructed Wills to stand guard in the lobby, in case burglars were in the building and tried to use that route to get away.

Leeper, Barrett, and Shoffler climbed the stairs to the office of the Federal Reserve Board on the eighth floor. They were met there by a Federal Reserve guard. The four of them turned on the lights and began searching all the rooms on the floor but found nothing.

From his lookout post, Baldwin spotted the lights being turned on and radioed Hunt at the Watergate Hotel, "The lights went on on the entire eighth floor."

At that point, Hunt made a grievously wrong assumption. "We know about that," he told Baldwin. "That is the two o'clock guard check. Let us know if anything else happens."

Hunt radioed Barker, "Be advised that the guard is making his two o'clock rounds on the eighth floor." Barker and the other burglars, accepting Hunt's premise that nothing more than a routine guard check was taking place two floors above them, were lulled into a false sense of security. They continued gathering documents and preparing to plant the "bug" in O'Brien's office.

The policemen now began searching other floors. Their suspicions were aroused when they found another strip of tape across the latch of the door leading from the staircase to the sixth floor, so they launched a cautious room-by-room check of the Democratic offices. Sergeant Leeper and Officer Shoffler, guns and flashlights in hand, walked onto a balcony outside the Democratic headquarters to search for suspects. From across

146

the street, Baldwin had a good view of them. He could see that one was wearing an Army jacket and the other a T-shirt, windbreaker, and golf cap. Behind them, in the office, he could see a third man with a gun.

Whispering into his walkie-talkie, Baldwin asked, "Any of your guys wearing hippie clothes?"

Gordon Liddy, with Hunt at the Watergate Hotel, grabbed a walkie-talkie and snapped, "Repeat."

"Any of your guys wearing hippie clothes?" Baldwin asked again.

"Negative," Liddy replied. "Our guys are in business suits. Why? Over."

"There's four, maybe five guys running around the sixth floor," Baldwin said. "Lights are going on. . . . Oh, oh, they've got guns. Looks like trouble."

"Keep reporting," Liddy ordered. Then he tried reaching the burglars by walkie-talkie. "One to two," he said. "Two, come in. There are lights on your floor. Any trouble?"

Receiving no response, Liddy tried again: "One to two, come in. This is an order. Repeat: come in!" Still, he got no answer.

The officers continued moving from room to room, shouting: "Come out! Police!" Realizing they had no escape route, the burglars knelt behind a wooden partition surrounding a secretary's desk—hoping the police would make an inadequate search and somehow miss them.

But within a short time, the policemen approached their hiding place. Officer Barrett spotted an arm sticking out from behind the partition. "Hold it!" he snapped. "Come out!" The burglars obeyed. Barker, the last to

147

rise, took the time before surrendering to whisper into his walkie-talkie, "They've got us!"

The officers, who quickly searched the suspects, sensed immediately that they had come upon no ordinary burglars. These men were wearing business suits. They had with them eavesdropping devices, other sophisticated electronic equipment, two cameras, and a walkie-talkie. Their pockets contained a total of more than $1,700 in cash, most of it in $100 bills. The burglars initially gave the police false names, matching those on the phony identification papers they were carrying. Shortly, a paddy wagon arrived to take them to a police station.

Meanwhile, Hunt and Liddy—realizing that the police would soon search their Watergate Hotel room because Barker had been carrying one of the room keys —hastily prepared to leave. They stuffed some of McCord's extra electronic equipment and other assorted paraphernalia into suitcases. Hunt radioed Baldwin to stay at the Howard Johnson's room until he got there. Liddy and Hunt carried the suitcases to Hunt's car, which was parked outside the hotel. By that time, additional policemen had converged outside the office building—a mere half block away—but they paid no heed to the two men with the suitcases.

Hunt drove Liddy four blocks, to his parked car, and dropped him off. They shook hands solemnly, with Liddy promising to call Hunt the following day. Hunt then turned around, drove to a point two blocks from the Watergate, parked and walked to the Howard Johnson's.

At the listening-post room, Hunt told Baldwin,

"Listen, it's all over. Pack up and get going." He explained that he wanted Baldwin to load all the potentially incriminating evidence in the room—including the radio receiver, other electronic equipment, walkie-talkie, typewriter, and tape recorders—into a panel truck McCord had bought for the Watergate operation and parked nearby. Baldwin was then to drive the truck to some place where he could leave it for safekeeping. After telling Baldwin he would receive further instructions at an unspecified future time, Hunt left.

Baldwin telephoned McCord's home in Rockville, Maryland, and told McCord's wife—who knew nothing about the political spying operation—that he was bringing the truck there. When he arrived, Baldwin told the bewildered, frightened Mrs. McCord little except that problems had developed on a job on which he had been working with her husband. At Baldwin's request, Mrs. McCord agreed to drive him back to Washington so that he could retrieve his car. When he left her, Baldwin drove directly to his hometown in Connecticut.

While Baldwin, Hunt, and Liddy scattered, the Washington police took their first tentative steps toward investigating the Watergate affair. Nobody had any way of knowing at the time how broadly the inquiry would spread—eventually attracting numerous other investigative agencies and rocking the very foundations of the United States government.

11 HIGH-LEVEL COVER-UP

Almost immediately after the arrest of the Watergate burglars, officials of the White House and the Committee for the Reelection of the President began trying to cover up the connections between the Nixon campaign and the break-in operation. This cover-up would become ever deeper and involve a widely growing number of officials. Investigation would ultimately reveal that President Nixon himself had played a leading role in devising and carrying out the cover-up strategy.

Within hours of the burglars' arrest, G. Gordon Liddy showed up at the CREEP office and began destroying his confidential files on the political-spying operation. Next, Liddy placed a long-distance call to Jeb Magruder, who had gone to Los Angeles with John

Mitchell and other top CREEP officials for meetings with California Republican leaders.

"Our security chief was arrested in the Democratic headquarters in the Watergate last night," Liddy said.

"What?" Magruder asked. "Do you mean McCord?"

"That's right, Jim McCord."

After hearing details of the arrests, Magruder bawled Liddy out for using McCord—who provided a direct connection between CREEP and the break-in—as a member of the burglary team. Liddy replied that he had not had sufficient time to find another wiretapper and thus had been compelled to use the only one available, McCord. "Don't worry," he told Magruder. "My men will never talk."

But Magruder *was* worried. He met with Mitchell and two other CREEP officials, Frederick LaRue and Robert C. Mardian, and briefed them on the arrests. The campaign officials decided it was urgent to get the five burglars released from police custody before investigators had a chance to draw from them any information linking the break-in to CREEP and the White House. Instructions were telephoned to Liddy to tell Richard Kleindienst, who had succeeded Mitchell as attorney general, that Mitchell wanted the burglars freed.

Liddy tracked Kleindienst down at a golf course, drew him aside in a locker room, and told him that Mitchell wanted the five men released from jail. Liddy also said the burglars might somehow be connected to CREEP or the White House. Kleindienst apparently did not believe the instructions came from Mitchell. In any event, he later said, he refused to abide by them;

151

instead, he immediately went to a phone and instructed Henry Petersen, the assistant attorney general in charge of the Justice Department's Criminal Division, to see that the Watergate burglars were treated just the same as any other defendants. Kleindienst did not, however, tell Petersen about the visit from Liddy—a visit that was clearly improper and probably violated the law against attempted obstruction of justice.

Meanwhile, E. Howard Hunt had also been concerned about the arrested men. Even after going to work with Liddy at CREEP, Hunt had retained his White House consultant's office. When he left Alfred Baldwin at the Howard Johnson's Motor Lodge on the night of the arrest, Hunt went directly to that office—in the Executive Office Building, adjacent to the White House. He unlocked the office safe and removed $10,000 in cash previously given him by Liddy for use in case any emergency should arise during the political-spying operation. Hunt placed in the safe a briefcase containing some of McCord's extra electronic gear that had been in the Watergate Hotel room.

Next, he telephoned a lawyer friend named C. Douglas Caddy, roused him from sleep, explained that he had an urgent problem to discuss, and asked if they could meet right away. Caddy told Hunt to come to his apartment. When he arrived shortly before 4 A.M., Hunt quickly described the arrest of the five men at the Democratic headquarters. He gave Caddy $8,500 of the money taken from the office safe, asking him to represent the arrested men and to try to get them bailed out of jail. "I want them out of jail and out of town before dawn," Hunt said.

Caddy said he would try to help and arranged for a Washington criminal lawyer named Joseph Rafferty, Jr., to join him in representing the burglars. Caddy and Rafferty visited the men at the jail and advised them they would be held in very high bail unless they gave the police their true names. Even after they had provided accurate identification, the defendants were ordered held on bail of $30,000 each—far too high to be covered by the money Hunt had given Caddy. Ultimately, they would remain in jail for more than a week while bail money was being raised.

The police, in searching the burglars after their arrest, had discovered keys to two rooms at the Watergate Hotel—the one that had been used by Hunt and Liddy as a command post and another that had been occupied by Frank Sturgis and Virgilio Gonzalez. After obtaining warrants, officers searched both rooms. They found, among other things, additional electronic equipment and another $3,566 in cash—most of it in consecutively numbered $100 bills. More important, they discovered several pieces of evidence connecting Hunt with the arrested men.

Within hours after the arrest of the burglars, FBI agents had joined Washington police in investigating the case. When Hunt's name cropped up, two FBI men went to his home to try to interview him. Hunt refused to answer their questions. Later he went to the White House and checked the contents of his office safe. He then visited the office of Charles Colson, President Nixon's special counsel, and told Colson's secretary to inform her boss: "That safe of mine upstairs is loaded [with incriminating material]."

153

Hunt was far from alone in his concern over incriminating evidence. Numerous White House and CREEP officials were worried about exposure of their roles in authorizing and planning the political-spying operation. They feared not only that such exposure could subject them to criminal prosecution, but also that it could endanger President Nixon's re-election chances.

While still in California, Jeb Magruder had telephoned his administrative assistant, Robert Reisner, in Washington, telling him to remove several files on the political-intelligence operation from Magruder's office. When Magruder returned to Washington, he retrieved the files. He later attended a meeting on the Watergate situation with John Mitchell and White House Counsel John Dean at Mitchell's apartment. Magruder says he asked Mitchell what he should do about the sensitive files and that Mitchell replied: "Maybe you ought to have a little fire at your house tonight." When he returned home, Magruder placed the files in his fireplace and burned them.

By June 19, two days after the arrest of the burglars, Nixon's chief domestic-affairs adviser, John Ehrlichman, had been placed in charge of the White House effort to limit its Watergate problems. Ehrlichman, Nixon's second-highest aide, enlisted Dean to help him. Dean says Ehrlichman instructed him to telephone Liddy and order him to get Hunt to leave the country.

Hunt says he received the message when, in response to a phone call from Liddy, he met him on a downtown Washington street. Liddy appeared tense, he says, and immediately told him: "They want you to get out of town. . . . Those are the orders. They want you to get moving, and fast."

"Where would I go?"

"How about Europe?" Liddy responded.

Hunt says that, although he was reluctant to leave the Washington area because he did not want to appear to be a fugitive, he agreed to get out of town—but not out of the country. He went home to pack. There, he received another call from Liddy, who told him the orders had been changed.

After briefly considering the change in instructions, Hunt says, he told Liddy:

> I don't know who's giving hard-and-fast orders, then rescinding them in forty-five minutes, Gordon, but I'll say this—it makes me uneasy. Obviously the decision to send me out of Washington had to be made with something approaching thought and wisdom. But then suddenly to cancel it makes me wonder what the hell's going on. . . . So I'm going to go up to New York this evening, and I'll get in touch with you from there.

He did go to New York, spent one night in a motel there, then flew to Los Angeles, and went into hiding at a friend's home.

Meanwhile, White House officials grew increasingly concerned that investigators might search Hunt's office safe and find incriminating evidence that could embarrass the president. At a White House meeting attended by Ehrlichman, Dean, and Colson, it was decided to open the safe and remove the contents.

155

Government experts drilled the safe open, and the contents were taken to Dean's office.

When Dean examined them, he found they included the briefcase containing some of McCord's surplus electronic eavesdropping equipment, a revolver and ammunition, and folder after folder of documents. Many of the documents related not only to Watergate but also to political dirty tricks and illegal operations by the White House Plumbers unit.

Dean immediately went to see Ehrlichman. Later, he gave the following account of their conversation: After hearing a description of the contents of Hunt's safe, Ehrlichman told Dean to shred the documents and "deep-six" the briefcase containing the electronic equipment. "What do you mean by deep-six?" Dean asked. Ehrlichman leaned back in his chair and said: "You drive across the [Potomac] river on your way home at night, don't you?" Dean acknowledged that he did, and Ehrlichman told him: "Well, when you cross over the bridge on your way home, just toss the briefcase into the river." Dean replied that Ehrlichman also crossed the river on his way home and that he could perform the distasteful chore. But Ehrlichman snapped: "No, thank you."

After mulling over Ehrlichman's "deep-six" suggestion for several days, Dean decided it would be imprudent. So many people were aware the safe had been emptied that there was no way of making sure the destruction of the contents could be kept secret. Instead, Dean sold Ehrlichman on an alternate plan. He would select some relatively harmless documents from Hunt's files and turn them over to FBI agents working on the Watergate investigation. The remainder of Hunt's materials would be given to Acting FBI Director L. Patrick Gray. Since Gray was a long-time Nixon political supporter and was eager to win appointment as permanent director of the FBI, he could be expected to handle the Hunt materials with discretion. And if Dean were ever called upon to testify about the contents of the safe, he could truthfully say they had been given to the FBI.

Two FBI men working on the Watergate case were called to the White House and given a batch of innocuous documents from Hunt's safe. The agents were led to believe the files represented the safe's entire contents. Then Gray was summoned to a meeting with Ehrlichman and Dean at Ehrlichman's office and was handed the sensitive materials from the safe. Gray eventually destroyed the documents and withheld word of their existence from his subordinates.

Nixon's chief aide, H. R. Haldeman, was also worried that his own files might contain potentially damaging documents. His assistant, Gordon Strachan, searched the files and brought Haldeman a stack of papers that could prove embarrassing. The documents included a memorandum referring to Liddy's political-spying program, plus reports on other political-espionage and dirty-tricks operations. "Make sure our files are clean," Haldeman told Strachan. Accordingly, Strachan ran the stack of documents through a shredding machine.

Meanwhile, President Nixon and White House and CREEP officials were deliberately misleading the public about the significance of the Watergate affair and who

157

had been behind it. White House Press Secretary Ron Ziegler tried to pass the case off as a "third-rate burglary attempt," not even worthy of comment. When the president was asked about it at a press conference five days after the arrests, he assured the American people that "the White House has no involvement whatever in this particular incident." On behalf of CREEP, John Mitchell issued a statement that misrepresented, among other things, McCord's role as the re-election committee's security director:

> We have learned from news reports that a man identified as employed by our campaign committee was one of five persons arrested at the Democratic National Committee headquarters. The person involved is the proprietor of a private security agency who was employed by our committee months ago to assist with the installation of our security system. He has, as we understand it, a number of business clients and interests and we have no knowledge of those relationships. We want to emphasize that this man and the other people involved were not operating either in our behalf or with our consent.

An important element of the White House cover-up involved trying to conceal the origin of the consecutively numbered $100 bills that had been found on the burglars and in their hotel rooms. Through the serial numbers, FBI agents had begun tracing the bills. White House officials knew the agents would eventually be able to determine that the money had come from the

CREEP finance committee. In an attempt to prevent such a disclosure, the officials—with the president's backing—tried to head off the investigation of the bills' origin.

The money had initially come to the finance committee as part of large, secret donations from campaign contributors. In efforts to maintain the secrecy of the contributions, the money had been "laundered"— passed through several bank accounts, including one in Mexico City, to make it more difficult to trace. The investigating FBI agents had come upon several checks written by campaign contributors during the laundering process. They wanted to question the contributors, but the White House officials were determined to prevent such interviews.

John Mitchell came up with an idea for cutting off the FBI investigation. As a former attorney general, Mitchell knew the FBI had a long-standing agreement with the CIA that neither agency would jeopardize the other's operations. If the FBI could be convinced that the CIA had somehow been involved in financing or carrying out the Watergate burglary, Mitchell reasoned, the investigation could be curtailed on the ground of protecting "national security." Mitchell suggested to John Dean that such an approach be considered.

Although the CIA had played no role in the Watergate operation, there were certain factors that lent an air of plausibility to the idea of its involvement: Both McCord and Hunt had formerly worked for the CIA, and some of the Cuban exiles arrested in the burglary had taken part in the CIA-directed Bay of Pigs.

159

Dean passed on Mitchell's suggestion to Haldeman, who discussed the idea with President Nixon on June 23:

> HALDEMAN: Now, on the investigation, you know the Democratic break-in thing, . . . Mitchell came up with yesterday and John Dean . . . concurs now with Mitchell's recommendation that the only way to solve this . . . is for us to have [Deputy CIA Director Vernon] Walters call Pat Gray and just say: "Stay to hell out of this—this is [our] business here; we don't want you to go any further on it." That's not an unusual development, and that would take care of it.
>
> NIXON: What about Pat Gray? You mean Pat Gray doesn't want to?
>
> HALDEMAN: Pat does want to. He doesn't know how to, and he doesn't have any basis for doing it. Given this, he will then have the basis. . . .
>
> NIXON: Yeah.

The president went on to give his full support to the cover-up plan. He told Haldeman: "They [CIA officials] should call the FBI in and [say], 'Don't go any further into this case, period.'"

Later that day, CIA Director Richard Helms and Deputy Director Walters were called to a White House meeting with Haldeman and John Ehrlichman. Haldeman explained that the president wanted Walters to tell Gray further investigation could compromise secret CIA operations. Helms pointed out he had told Gray only one day earlier that the CIA had no connection with the Watergate affair. But Haldeman persisted, and Helms and Walters reluctantly agreed to go along with the plan.

Walters went directly from the White House to see Gray. After telling Gray that he had just come from talking to "senior staff members" at the White House, Walters reminded him of the agreement that the FBI and CIA would protect each other's operations. He said the FBI was likely to "uncover some CIA assets or sources" if it pursued its investigation of the Watergate money. Gray said later he took Walters to mean that the CIA had some sort of interest in the money involved and that further FBI investigation of the matter would reveal secret CIA operations. He told Walters that the Watergate case was "a most awkward matter to come up during an election year" but assured him that the FBI would handle the investigation "in a manner that would not hamper the CIA."

After Walters left, Gray instructed his subordinates not to interview the campaign contributors who had signed the checks used in laundering the money. His order temporarily cut off investigation of the origin of the $100 bills.

During the next few days, Walters began having second thoughts about allowing the CIA to be drawn into the cover-up plan. He conferred with several subordinates who emphasized that no secret CIA operations could possibly be exposed by a full FBI investigation of the Watergate money. His doubts were heightened when he was called to a meeting on June 26 with John Dean, who told him the White House wanted still more help from the CIA on its Watergate

161

problems. Dean said some of the arrested burglars "were wobbling and might talk." Walters replied: "That is just too bad, but it has nothing to do with us because nothing that they can say can implicate the agency [CIA]."

At the FBI, meantime, some of Gray's aides complained bitterly that the bureau was being drawn into a cover-up. They urged Gray to order an immediate resumption of the investigation into the Watergate money. At one point, Gray instructed his subordinates to go ahead with the interviews of the campaign contributors. But within a few hours, under pressure from John Dean, he rescinded the instruction.

That decision created still further resentment among Gray's aides. Under additional prodding from them, Gray concluded that he could not hold up the investigation any longer in the absence of a letter from the CIA requesting that he do so. He asked for such a letter from Walters in a meeting on July 5, but Walters refused to provide it: "Such a letter in the current atmosphere of Washington would become known prior to election day and what was now a minor wound could become a mortal wound."

Walters and Gray had no way of knowing that Nixon had been personally involved in devising the plan to use the CIA to curb the FBI investigation. They wrongly assumed the decision had been made by his aides, without the president's knowledge. They decided the president should be warned that he was being done a disservice—if not worse—by his subordinates.

Gray reached Nixon by telephone and told him: "Walters and I feel that people on your staff are trying to mortally wound you by using the CIA and FBI and by confusing the questions of CIA interest in, or not in, people the FBI wishes to interview." Gray fully expected Nixon would ask for more information on who was trying to "mortally wound" him and precisely how it was being done. But instead, he said only: "Pat, you just continue to conduct your aggressive and thorough investigation." The conversation ended abruptly at that point, and Gray never received any future inquiries from Nixon on the matter.

Gray then ordered his subordinates to resume the investigation into the Watergate money. Agents were finally sent to interview the campaign contributors, who provided additional information on the origin of the $100 bills. By that time, the FBI had uncovered evidence indicating that Gordon Liddy had played a role in the Watergate operation. Agents tried to interview him, but he refused to answer any of their questions. CREEP officials, realizing that Liddy was bound to become an increasing source of embarrassment, used his refusal to cooperate with the FBI as an excuse for firing him.

But Liddy's dismissal did not, by any means, end the problems he posed for CREEP and the White House. By the time of the Watergate arrests, the campaign organizations had given him $199,000 of the $250,000 budgeted for his political-spying project. The CREEP officials doubted the FBI agents would believe Liddy had been given that much money for strictly legal purposes. Although Liddy had some duties other than political spying, those duties would not have required any expenditure approaching that amount. Thus

163

it was decided to try to concoct a story that Liddy had been given far less money—all of it designated for use on perfectly legal projects.

Jeb Magruder approached campaign treasurer Hugh Sloan, who had turned over much of the money to Liddy. Magruder said problems would arise if Sloan gave FBI agents an accurate accounting of the money allocated to Liddy. He proposed initially that Sloan claim Liddy had received only $75,000 to $80,000. Sloan told him: "I have no intention of perjuring myself." Magruder replied: "You may have to." But Sloan continued to resist the suggestion, and the meeting broke up without agreement.

Extremely disturbed by Magruder's request, Sloan went to top CREEP and White House officials and complained that something was radically wrong inside the Nixon campaign. But the officials—including Mitchell and Ehrlichman—shrugged off his warnings. He was told he had been working too hard and should take a vacation. He did so. But immediately upon his return, Magruder resumed pressing him to lie about the money given to Liddy. This time, he suggested Sloan go to the federal prosecutor heading the Watergate investigation and tell him Liddy had received only $40,000 to $45,000. Sloan agreed to think over the proposal. The next day Sloan told Magruder that, if questioned by the authorities, he intended to provide an accurate accounting of the money given to Liddy.

Next, Sloan went to see two lawyers who had been retained to represent CREEP in all matters arising from the Watergate case. He told them everything he knew, including the story of Magruder's attempts to persuade

164

him to lie. The lawyers suggested he leave Washington temporarily. A short time later, Sloan received a telephone call from CREEP official Fred LaRue instructing him in even stronger terms to leave the capital immediately. Sloan flew to California. But after six days, he returned to Washington and met with LaRue, who suggested he plead the Fifth Amendment against self-incrimination if called to testify in the investigation. Sloan refused, resigned his job at CREEP, went to the federal prosecutors, and offered to cooperate with them.

While Sloan had been in California, CREEP officials had put together a substitute phony story about the money given to Liddy. Magruder would claim he had given about half the funds to Liddy to conduct legitimate investigations required for the campaign. To account for the other half, Magruder enlisted the help of a young CREEP official named Herbert Porter. After working in the White House communications office, Porter had become scheduling director for CREEP. His duties included supervising a so-called surrogate speakers' program in which leading Republicans delivered campaign speeches throughout the country on Nixon's behalf. At Magruder's request, Porter agreed to tell investigators he had turned over about $100,000 to Liddy. He would say the money was to be used for hiring college students to infiltrate and provide information on radical organizations suspected of planning demonstrations against Nixon and the surrogate speakers. Eventually, Porter and Magruder told their false stories to FBI agents, federal prosecutors, and a grand jury investigating the Watergate case.

These stories were part of a broader plan for cover-

165

ing up true responsibility for the Watergate affair. That plan called for persuading investigators and the public that, if Liddy had used CREEP funds to finance the Watergate operation, he had done so without the knowledge or consent of CREEP and White House officials. In short, it would be claimed that Liddy—for reasons known only to himself—had embarked on an unauthorized adventure of his own. The strategy was aimed at ensuring that the focus of the investigation was limited to Liddy, Hunt, and the five burglars.

Meanwhile, John Mitchell resigned as head of CREEP. Although the Watergate affair unquestionably played a role in his decision, he did not mention it in his letter of resignation to the president. Instead, he said he was quitting because his outspoken wife, Martha, had threatened to leave him if he did not get out of politics. He was succeeded in the top post at CREEP by Clark MacGregor, the White House director of congressional relations. Even after resigning, however, Mitchell continued to play a leading role in the cover-up. He met frequently with Magruder and LaRue to refine the cover-up plan. At times, John Dean sat in on the meetings.

Dean played an important part in maintaining the cover-up by riding herd on the investigation at the White House. He insisted on being present, in his capacity as legal counsel to the president, at all FBI interviews of White House employees. Normally, only FBI agents and the people being questioned attend such interviews.

Through Dean's intercession, White House officials were spared from appearing in person before the grand jury investigating the Watergate case. Dean told Justice Department officials that unfair publicity, potentially harmful to Nixon's re-election campaign, might result if the White House officials were seen entering the grand-jury room by news reporters. A procedure was worked out in which the officials were questioned privately under oath by federal prosecutors at Justice Department headquarters. Their testimony was then read to the grand jury. This system, of course, prevented the grand jurors from asking their own questions of the witnesses.

On another front, Dean prevailed upon Henry Petersen, the assistant attorney general overseeing the case for the Justice Department, to place sharp limits on the investigation. Dean told Petersen he "did not think the White House could withstand a wide-open investigation." He urged that the inquiry be restricted merely to the facts of the burglary itself—rather than examining the broader political implications. Petersen responded by telling the prosecutors handling the case: "Keep your eye on the mark. . . . We're not investigating the whole damn political thing."

President Nixon, meanwhile, contributed further to the cover-up by issuing a series of statements assuring the public that there had been no White House involvement in the Watergate affair. In one such statement, for example, Nixon said:

Within our own staff, under my direction, Counsel to the President, Mr. Dean, has conducted a complete investigation of all leads which might involve any present members of the White House

167

or anybody in the government. I can say categorically that his investigation indicates that no one in the White House staff, no one in this administration, presently employed, was involved in this very bizarre incident.

Actually, Dean had conducted no such investigation and had given him no such assurances.

From all indications, the cover-up seemed to be succeeding. When the grand jury returned its indictments in the Watergate case on September 15, the defendants cited were limited to the five burglars, Liddy, and Hunt. They were charged with burglary, conspiracy, and illegal wiretapping. A Justice Department spokesman announced that the investigation had ended and that "we have absolutely no evidence that any others should be charged."

Shortly after learning of the grand jury action, Nixon met with Dean and Haldeman at the White House. The president congratulated Dean on his success in limiting the investigation and thus preventing it from hurting Nixon during the re-election campaign.

But White House and CREEP officials knew they were not completely out of the woods. There was still the danger that the cover-up might be destroyed if one or more of the indicted defendants decided to talk, exposing the roles in the Watergate affair played by higher-ups. In efforts to prevent such disclosures, the officials had already taken action to encourage the indicted men to remain silent. They had secretly begun paying hush money to the defendants—money the men used for attorneys' fees, living expenses, and other purposes. Now, the officials recognized, they would have to continue making such payoffs at least through the election and probably even afterward.

John Dean had initially tried to arrange for the CIA to provide financial support to the defendants. After the CIA refused, Dean discussed the matter with John Mitchell. Agreeing that payments should be made to the men, Mitchell suggested that Dean seek his White House superiors' approval to use Nixon's personal attorney, Herbert Kalmbach, to raise the necessary money. Kalmbach had been a highly successful fund raiser for Nixon's election campaigns and had served for a time as deputy finance chairman of CREEP.

Dean discussed Mitchell's proposal with H. R. Haldeman and John Ehrlichman, who approved giving Kalmbach the assignment. Dean met with Kalmbach and falsely assured him that the payments were legal, but he cautioned that secrecy was necessary. If word of the payments leaked out, he said, the public might misunderstand. Although he had some misgivings, Kalmbach agreed to take on the assignment. Dean suggested he use Anthony Ulasewicz, a former New York City policeman who had conducted confidential investigations for the White House, to deliver the money to the defendants.

Kalmbach started out by using funds provided by CREEP. Maurice Stans, chairman of the CREEP finance committee, gave him $75,000 in $100 bills with which to begin paying the hush money. Kalmbach turned the cash over to Ulasewicz.

Arrangements were made for Hunt's wife, Dorothy, to deal with Ulasewicz on behalf not only of her hus-

169

band but also of the other defendants. Ulasewicz asked Mrs. Hunt to get all seven defendants to estimate their living expenses, legal fees, and other costs for the next five months—a span that would stretch beyond the election. After conferring with the defendants, Mrs. Hunt told Ulasewicz by telephone that the total would come to more than $400,000. Since Ulasewicz did not have anywhere near that much money on hand, he agreed to make a down payment of $40,000, which was to be divided among the defendants.

Ulasewicz stashed the money, inside a zippered airline travel bag, in a locker at Washington National Airport. He taped the key to the locker beneath the coin box of a nearby telephone booth. Acting on telephoned instructions from Ulasewicz, Mrs. Hunt went to the phone booth at a designated time, picked up the key, then collected the money from the locker. Ulasewicz watched from a discreet distance as the pickup was made. Mrs. Hunt later distributed shares of the money to her husband and his six codefendants.

With the original supply of hush money almost depleted, Kalmbach obtained another $40,000 from CREEP. But John Dean told him that CREEP was running short of cash and that he would have to begin raising money from outside sources for future payments to the defendants. By that time, Kalmbach was having serious doubts about whether such payments were proper. Seeking to set these doubts at rest, he went to the White House to see John Ehrlichman.

"John, I am looking right into your eyes," Kalmbach said. "I know Jeanne [Mrs. Ehrlichman] and your family; you know Barbara [Mrs. Kalmbach] and my family. You know my family and my reputation mean everything to me. And it's just absolutely necessary, John, that you tell me that John Dean has the authority to direct me in this assignment, that it is a proper assignment and that I am to go forward in it."

"Herb, John Dean does have the authority," Ehrlichman told him. "It is proper, and you are to go forward." While claiming the payments to the defendants were proper, however, Ehrlichman emphasized the necessity of keeping them secret. If news reporters learned about them, he told Kalmbach, "they'd have our heads in their laps."

Reassured, at least temporarily, Kalmbach agreed to begin trying to raise outside money for the operation. He went to see an old friend and long-time political contributor, Thomas V. Jones, board chairman of the Northrop Corporation, an aircraft manufacturing firm that depended heavily on government contracts. Jones gave him a $75,000 donation from Northrop funds. He would later say he understood the money was to be a contribution to the Nixon re-election campaign and that he knew nothing about the special fund for the defendants. Even if the contribution had gone to the Nixon campaign, it would have been illegal, since federal law prohibited donation of corporate funds to national political campaigns.

Kalmbach met Ulasewicz in California and gave him the $75,000 for distribution to the defendants. During their meeting, Kalmbach—experiencing fresh doubts about the propriety of the hush-money payments— sought Ulasewicz's advice. "Tony, what's your opinion of all this?" he asked. Ulasewicz gave him a blunt re-

171

sponse. "Well, Mr. Kalmbach, I will tell you, something here is not kosher. It's definitely not your ball game, Mr. Kalmbach."

Even though he felt that way, Ulasewicz continued distributing the hush money. Kalmbach, troubled by the secrecy he was required to maintain, brooded over the advice Ulasewicz had given him about the payments not being "kosher." Finally, in late August, Kalmbach told John Dean and CREEP official Fred LaRue that he had decided the payoff operation was improper and that he could no longer take part in it. At a later meeting, he gave Dean and LaRue a full accounting of the money taken in and distributed. The $29,900 left in the payoff fund was transferred over to LaRue, who was to take over responsibility for both raising and distributing future hush-money payments.

Soon afterward, some of the defendants—most notably Hunt—started grumbling that CREEP was not fulfilling its financial promises to them. Through intermediaries, the complaints were forwarded to Dean. Fearing that one or more of the disgruntled defendants might blow the lid off the cover-up and hurt Nixon's re-election campaign, Dean sent back word that the promises would be kept. A short time later, following orders from John Mitchell, LaRue went to Florida and obtained $50,000 from one of Nixon's closest friends, Charles G. (Bebe) Rebozo. Part of that money was then passed on to Hunt's lawyer, William Bittman.

Although that payment still left many of the financial promises unmet, it served the purpose of temporarily assuring the defendants that they were not being abandoned by the committee and the White House. They continued to complain privately, but they kept silent publicly. Thus the cover-up was maintained through the election.

The Democrats had chosen as their presidential nominee Senator George McGovern of South Dakota, regarded by the Nixon forces as the weakest candidate among the leading Democratic contenders. McGovern tried to make the Watergate affair a major campaign issue. But partly as a result of the cover-up, he achieved little success. The public and press generally gave short shrift to his attempts to hold Nixon personally responsible for Watergate. On election day, Nixon swept to a landslide victory—capturing all the electoral votes except those of Massachusetts and the District of Columbia. His margin in popular votes, more than 47 million to McGovern's 29 million, was the largest in the nation's history.

Following the election, the Watergate defendants stepped up their pressure for payment of the money they had been promised. They were afraid that White House and CREEP officials, with the election safely won, might lose interest in helping them. Acting as their spokesman, Hunt made clear that dire consequences might befall the Nixon camp if they were abandoned. He telephoned Nixon's special counsel, Charles Colson, an old friend who had originally sponsored him for his job as a White House consultant:

Commitments that were made to all of us at the onset have not been kept. And there's a great deal of unease and concern on the part of seven defendants. . . . After all, we're protecting the

173

guys who were really responsible. . . . But, at the same time, this is a two-way street and we think that now is the time when some moves should be made and surely your cheapest commodity available is money.

Colson expressed sympathy for the defendants' plight but made no promises. Unknown to Hunt, Colson had tape-recorded the conversation and later played it for Dean, Haldeman, and Ehrlichman. Haldeman and Ehrlichman instructed Dean to tell John Mitchell "to take care of all these problems." Dean passed the word, but Mitchell took no immediate action.

Hunt then wrote a memorandum spelling out the defendant's complaints in greater detail. He accused the White House of, among other things, "an apparent wash-hands attitude now that the election has been won, heightening the sense of unease among all defendants, who have grown increasingly to feel that they are being offered up as scapegoats ultimately to be abandoned." The memorandum went on to threaten that the defendants might make damaging disclosures if they did not receive satisfactory responses to their complaints.

Hunt wrote that the defendants were able to provide testimony showing that "Mitchell may well have perjured himself." He also noted that congressional elections would take place in two years and that evidence provided by the defendants could seriously damage the Republican cause. The memorandum warned that the defendants would meet on November 25 "to determine our joint and automatic response to evidence of continued indifference on the part of those in whose behalf we have suffered the loss of our employment, our futures and our reputations as honorable men."

Hunt gave the memorandum to his lawyer, William Bittman, who read it to CREEP attorney Kenneth Parkinson. The contents were quickly relayed to White House and CREEP officials. Bittman then gave Parkinson a list of the defendants' latest financial demands, which was forwarded to LaRue and Dean. Again, the Nixon camp turned to Mitchell for a solution to its problems with the defendants. This time, Mitchell acted.

Since there was no other cash available to meet the defendants' demands, Mitchell told Dean to make use of a secret fund maintained at the White House by Haldeman. The fund, originally amounting to $350,000 left over from Nixon's 1968 presidential campaign, had been entrusted to Haldeman by CREEP in February 1972. Ostensibly, it was to be used for such purposes as conducting confidential public opinion polls for the White House. Actually, it could be used for any emergency that might arise. By November there was $328,000 left. With Haldeman's approval, $50,000 was removed and given to LaRue, who passed it along to Bittman.

In early December, a United Airlines plane on a flight from Washington crashed while trying to land in thick fog at Chicago's Midway Airport. Among the forty-three persons aboard the plane killed in the crash was Hunt's wife, Dorothy. Investigators searching the wreckage found Mrs. Hunt's purse, which contained $10,000 in cash. Hunt later explained that his wife was on her way to visit relatives in Chicago and had planned to invest the money in a hotel-management company the relatives owned. Although there was speculation that Mrs. Hunt had actually been on a mission to deliver hush money to one of her husband's codefendants, no proof was ever produced to support such a theory. Similarly, there were allegations that sabotage —somehow related to the Watergate case—had caused the plane crash. But no evidence of such sabotage was found, and government investigators ruled that the crash had been an accident.

In any event, his wife's death sent Hunt into a deep depression. He and the other Watergate defendants were scheduled to stand trial in little more than a month. All had pleaded not guilty when originally arraigned after their indictment. But now a despondent Hunt, reluctant to go through the ordeal of a prolonged trial in the aftermath of his wife's death, began talking about changing his plea to guilty. He coupled such talk, however, with expressions of hope—not to mention expectation—that he would be granted leniency. Specifically, he felt President Nixon owed it to him to order him released as quickly as possible if he should be given a stiff prison sentence.

Under the Constitution, the president has the power to grant pardons and reprieves to federal prisoners— no matter how serious the crimes they have committed. The process involved is commonly known as the granting of executive clemency. A president's decision to award executive clemency cannot be overruled by the courts or the Congress.

When Nixon discussed the situation by telephone with Colson on January 8, he made it clear he was prepared to approve clemency for Hunt himself. "[On the] question of clemency, Hunt's is a simple case," Nixon told Colson. "I mean, after all, the man's wife is dead, was killed." He even went as far as to suggest that the White House could prepare the public for news of the granting of clemency to Hunt by arranging for a nationally syndicated newspaper columnist to write an article calling for such action. As for Hunt's codefendants, however, Nixon told Colson he would "have difficulty" with giving them all clemency.

> COLSON: Well, the others aren't going to get the same. The vulnerabilities are different.
> NIXON: Why?
> COLSON: Well, because Hunt and Liddy did the work. The others didn't know any direct information [damaging to the White House and CREEP]. . . .
> NIXON: Well, I think I agree.
> COLSON: See, I don't give a damn if they [the other defendants] spend five years in jail. They can't hurt us. Hunt and Liddy—direct meetings, discussions are very incriminating to us.

Three days after that conversation, Hunt pleaded guilty. His sentencing was postponed until the cases against the other defendants had been decided. Meanwhile, Hunt conferred with the four Miami men he had recruited for the Watergate operation. Bernard Barker said he and the three others had decided to follow Hunt's lead and plead guilty. "The evidence against us is overwhelming," Barker said. "We were caught on the [Watergate] premises and you weren't. If you're pleading guilty, then that's enough for us." On January 15 Barker, Frank Sturgis, Eugenio Martinez, and Virgilio Gonzalez changed their pleas to guilty. Their sentencings were also postponed.

Thus only Gordon Liddy and James McCord were left to be tried. Both made clear they had no intention of pleading guilty. Liddy, a fanatic supporter of the Nixon cause, was expected to maintain silence about Watergate and the cover-up even if convicted and given a long prison sentence. McCord, however, was considered a threat by White House and CREEP officials.

While awaiting trial, McCord privately sent word to government officials that he was extremely disturbed over being left to "take the rap" with his codefendants for higher-ups who had approved the Watergate operation. He was also upset about repeated attempts to place the blame for Watergate on the CIA. McCord says that a few weeks before his scheduled trial, his own defense attorney, Gerald Alch, returned from a meeting with Hunt's lawyer and suggested McCord base his defense on a claim that Watergate was a CIA operation. He says Alch proposed that he maintain he had been called out of retirement by the CIA to tap the Democrats' phone lines. McCord refused to adopt such a defense: ". . . I would not turn on the organization that had employed me for nineteen years. . . . I . . . would not let anyone wrongly lay the operation at the feet of the CIA."

McCord wrote a series of letters to former colleagues still with the CIA warning that attempts were being made to blame the agency for Watergate. He suggested

178

that CIA officials try to head off these efforts by leaking word about them to the news media. His letters also said he was in a position to expose the roles of higher-ups in the Watergate affair. One, for example, noted: "I have the evidence of the involvement of Mitchell and others, sufficient to convene a jury, the Congress and the press." Still, Alch continued to press McCord to adopt the CIA defense.

By that time, McCord had stopped accepting hush money in order, as he put it, "to be completely free to pursue whatever course of action my conscience dictated without being obligated." Now, he decided to send a clear message to the White House that he would not stand idly by if the attempts persisted to blame Watergate on the CIA. He wrote a letter to John (Jack) Caulfield, a former New York City policeman who had become a White House aide and then had been appointed assistant director of the Treasury Department's Alcohol, Tobacco and Firearms Division. Caulfield, who had carried out confidential investigations while working at the White House, had originally recommended McCord for the job as CREEP security director. McCord's letter to Caulfield said:

Dear Jack:
I'm sorry to have to write you this letter, but felt you had to know. If . . . the Watergate operation is laid at CIA's feet, where it does not belong, every tree in the forest will fall. It will be a scorched desert. The whole matter is at the precipice now. Just pass the message that, if they want

179

it to blow, they are on exactly the right course. I'm sorry that you will get hurt in the fallout.

As McCord had expected, Caulfield took the letter to the White House. He gave it to John Dean, who soon relayed word of its contents to John Mitchell. A short time later, Alch halted his attempt to persuade McCord to use the CIA story as a defense. Meanwhile, Mitchell told Dean that McCord should be offered the identical guarantee of executive clemency given to Hunt.

Dean instructed Caulfield to meet with McCord and impress on him the importance of accepting the clemency offer. Following telephoned instructions, McCord met Caulfield at a scenic overlook near the Potomac. McCord says Caulfield told him the clemency guarantee came from "the very highest levels of the White House" and that President Nixon would get a personal report on their meeting.

McCord did not seem impressed. He said he was "not like" the other defendants and that he had no interest in receiving executive clemency. Nor would he agree to plead guilty and remain silent about the cover-up. But he described to Caulfield a bizarre plan he had for forcing the government to drop its case against him. McCord had reason to believe the FBI was tapping the telephones of the Israeli and Chilean embassies in Washington. While awaiting trial, he had made calls to both embassies. He had not given his name but had said he was involved in the Watergate case and wanted to obtain visas to visit Israel and Chile. McCord was convinced that the FBI wiretaps had picked up both conversations. He hoped the prosecutors would privately admit as much. If they would, he told Caulfield, the government would be confronted with the possibility of having to concede publicly at the trial that it had tapped the embassy phones. To avoid such an embarrassing revelation—which would be bound to damage the nation's dealings with Chile and Israel—McCord suggested that the prosecutors dismiss the charges against him. He asked Caulfield to sound out government officials on the question.

Caulfield reported on the discussion to Dean, who told him to keep McCord happy by telling him they were checking out the conversations with the embassies. Actually, though, neither Dean nor other government officials gave serious consideration to McCord's plan. Caulfield followed the instructions when he met with McCord two days later. He also told McCord the government's well-being depended on his cooperation.

> The President's ability to govern is at stake. The government may fall. Everybody else is on track but you. You are not following the game plan. Get closer to your attorney. You seem to be pursuing your own course of action. Don't talk if called before the grand jury, keep silent, and do the same if called before a congressional committee.

McCord replied angrily that he had "no intention of either pleading guilty, taking executive clemency, or agreeing to remain silent." He said a major injustice was being done—that he and his codefendants were being prosecuted while such men as Mitchell, Magruder, and Dean "were going to be covered for." The meeting ended without any agreement.

Caulfield and McCord later talked several times by telephone and met once more. McCord continued to resist offers of executive clemency and financial support if sent to prison. Caulfield asked what he planned to do about exposing the cover-up. McCord said he planned to speak out publicly when he was ready but did not say when that would be. Caulfield replied:

> Jim, I have worked with these [White House] people and I know them to be as tough-minded as you and I. When you make your statement, don't underestimate them. . . . You know that, if the administration gets its back to the wall, it will have to take steps to defend itself.

McCord says he took Caulfield's comments as a personal threat. He replied that he had lived a good life, that his will was made out, that he had thought through the risks and would take them when he was ready.

At the trial of McCord and Liddy, however, neither McCord nor anyone else blew the whistle on the cover-up. The prosecution contended that the Watergate conspiracy had begun and ended with the seven arrested defendants. Chief prosecutor Earl Silbert described Liddy as "the leader of the conspiracy . . . the boss." He said there could have been no higher-ups involved, since Liddy and McCord "were off on an enterprise of their own."

Presiding Judge John J. Sirica made it clear he did not believe that the whole story was being told. Dissatisfied with the questions being asked by the opposing lawyers, Sirica frequently interrupted with questions of his own. For example, he told Bernard Barker: "I want to know where the money comes from. There were $100 bills floating around like coupons." When Barker responded that he had received his money "in the mail in a blank envelope," the judge told him: "I'm sorry, I don't believe you." Defense lawyers complained that the judge's questions were intruding on the prerogatives of the opposing attorneys, but Sirica set aside their objections: "I don't think we [judges] should sit up here like nincompoops. The function of a trial is to search for the truth."

But the whole truth clearly did not emerge at the trial. Jeb Magruder and Herbert Porter stuck to their stories that the money provided Liddy by CREEP had been intended for strictly legitimate projects. They denied that Watergate had been a CREEP operation. The chief prosecution witness was Alfred Baldwin, who had served as a lookout for the burglars and monitored the Watergate wiretaps. Baldwin, who had been given immunity from prosecution in return for his testimony, described the defendants' participation in the affair. But he knew nothing about the involvement of higher-ups. The trial ended on January 30 with the jury's verdict that Liddy and McCord were guilty on all counts.

Judge Sirica, who postponed sentencing all the Watergate defendants until March, said after hearing the verdict: "I have not been satisfied, and I am still not satisfied, that all the pertinent facts that might be available—I say *might* be available—have been produced before an American jury."

Sirica was far from alone in feeling that significant sections of the Watergate story had not yet been told. Several newspaper reporters—most notably Bob Woodward and Carl Bernstein of the *Washington Post* —had written stories charging that responsibility for Watergate went far beyond the seven defendants to White House and CREEP officials. They also published articles about dirty tricks pulled by Donald Segretti and others on behalf of the Nixon campaign. Despite repeated White House denials of such stories—using such terms as "shabby journalism" and a "senseless pack of lies"—the suspicion lingered in many quarters that much remained to be known about the Watergate case.

Senator Edward Kennedy of Massachusetts began a preliminary investigation of his own, aided by the staff of his Subcommittee on Administrative Practices and Procedures. The evidence gathered in Kennedy's inquiry helped convince Senate Democratic leaders that an extensive public investigation was needed.

Senate Majority Leader Mike Mansfield of Montana told a caucus of Democratic senators: "The so-called Watergate affair appears to have been nothing less than a callous attempt to subvert the political process of the nation in blatant disregard of the law." Mansfield said Watergate and related dirty tricks "warranted attention" from the Senate.

Finally, on February 7, the Senate agreed by a vote of 77 to 0 to establish a Select Committee on Presi-

184

dential Campaign Activities. The committee was authorized "to conduct an investigation and study of the extent, if any, to which illegal, improper or unethical activities were engaged in by any persons, acting individually or in combination with others, in the presidential election of 1972 or any campaign, canvass or other activity related to it."

In particular, the committee was empowered to investigate the planning and carrying out of the Watergate operation and whether there was evidence of a conspiracy to cover it up. It was also assigned to check on any other dirty tricks that might have been played during the 1972 presidential campaign. The committee was authorized to conduct televised hearings, and it was given a $500,000 appropriation to support a large staff of attorneys, investigators, researchers, and backup personnel.

The Watergate cover-up was about to confront its sternest test.

12 A NATION IN TORMENT

Democratic Senator Sam Ervin of North Carolina was appointed chairman of the Senate Select Committee on Presidential Campaign Activities, which would soon come to be called simply the Senate Watergate Committee. At the age of seventy-six, Ervin was one of the Senate's most highly respected members. Although he delighted in describing himself as "just an old country lawyer," he was a graduate of Harvard Law School and an acknowledged expert on constitutional law. He had served six years as a county judge and seven years on the North Carolina Superior Court before beginning the first of his three six-year terms in the Senate. An ardent civil libertarian, he became perhaps the leading congressional spokesman against government intrusion on citizens' rights. With his folksy manner and his ability to cut to the heart of an issue, he would ultimately evolve into a political folk hero of sorts through the Watergate committee's televised hearings.

Republican Senator Howard Baker of Tennessee was named as the committee's vice-chairman. Other members of the committee were Democrats Herman Talmadge of Georgia, Joseph Montoya of New Mexico, and Daniel Inouye of Hawaii, and Republicans Lowell Weicker of Connecticut and Edward Gurney of Florida.

Soon after the committee was appointed, White House officials met to plan their tactics for dealing with the new investigation. John Dean, one of those attending the meeting, says the following strategy was adopted:

> The White House will take a public posture of full cooperation but privately will attempt to restrain the investigation and make it as difficult as possible to get information and witnesses. A behind-the-scenes media effort would be made to make the Senate inquiry appear very partisan. The ultimate goal would be to discredit the hearings and reduce their impact. . . .

After choosing its staff, Senator Ervin's committee began its work by interviewing potential witnesses who would later be questioned at private hearings and ultimately, if their testimony was sufficiently important, at the televised public hearings. The committee served notice that it intended to call as witnesses various present and former White House officials.

President Nixon quickly moved to try to block such

testimony. He issued a statement invoking the controversial doctrine of executive privilege, which he claimed protected White House aides from being compelled to testify before congressional committees. The central theme of the statement was that White House officials would not feel free to offer candid advice to the president if they knew they might later be called to justify such advice in congressional testimony. Accordingly, Nixon said, he would forbid present and former White House aides to testify before the Watergate committee or any other congressional committee.

His statement touched off a storm of controversy. Many legal experts said the president had no right to issue such a broad-scale ban on testimony by his aides. Some said that the doctrine of executive privilege, even if valid, was meant to apply to limited confidential items and could not be used to justify such a sweeping order as Nixon's. Others argued that the doctrine was not valid. Harvard Law School Professor Raoul Berger, considered perhaps the nation's leading authority on executive privilege, said "executive privilege—root and branch—is a myth, without constitutional basis." Still other critics noted that Nixon himself, while a congressman, had adamantly protested President Harry S Truman's use of executive privilege in withholding an FBI report from a congressional committee.

Members of the Watergate committee unanimously took the position that executive privilege could not be used to cover up possible criminal acts. They indicated they were prepared to go to court, if necessary, to compel White House aides to testify. But first, attempts would be made to reach a compromise with Nixon.

While the issue of executive privilege hung in abeyance, other problems developed for the White House. The sentencing date for the seven Watergate defendants, March 23, was fast approaching, and E. Howard Hunt began making stiff new demands for money. Hunt says he wanted to make financial arrangements for the care of his children before the sentencing, in case Judge Sirica should send him to prison.

On March 16 Hunt met with CREEP attorney Paul O'Brien and complained that financial promises made to him had not been fulfilled. He demanded a $132,000 payment before his sentencing—$60,000 for back legal fees and the remainder to support his family for the next two years. Hunt also gave O'Brien a message to relay to John Dean. The message, a none too veiled threat, was that Hunt had done "seamy things" for the White House and would be forced to "review his options" if his financial demands were not met. Later, through another intermediary, Hunt sent even stronger word to the White House: If he did not get the demanded money, he said, he would see to it that the Republicans lost the 1974 and 1976 elections.

When the messages reached Dean, he brooded over what he regarded as a worsening White House crisis over Watergate. He saw the administration being dragged ever deeper into a morass from which there would be no easy escape. The demands for hush money might run on indefinitely. And there was the constant danger that one or more links in the cover-up chain might break, blowing the whole story into the open.

Dean decided to review the entire situation with Nixon. At 10:12 A.M. on March 21, Dean entered the

Oval Office and began providing the fullest report he had thus far given the president on the Watergate affair and the hazards that lay ahead:

I think that there is no doubt about the seriousness of the problem we've got. We have a cancer within, close to the presidency, that is growing. It is growing daily. It's compounded, growing geometrically now, because it compounds itself. . . . Basically, it is because (1) we are being blackmailed; (2) people are going to start perjuring themselves very quickly that have not had to perjure themselves [in the past] to protect other people in the line. And there is no assurance—

"That that won't bust?" the president interjected, and Dean agreed. He went on to describe at length the details of the cover-up. "It will cost money. It is dangerous," Dean said. Then Nixon asked how much Dean needed for the hush money.

Dean replied, "I would say these people are going to cost a million dollars over the next two years." He later explained that "these people" referred to all the Watergate defendants except McCord, who was still refusing to accept further hush money. He also described Hunt's most recent demand for $132,000.

NIXON: On the money, if you need the money, you could get that. You could get a million dollars. You could get it in cash. I know where it could be gotten. It is not easy, but it could be

190

done. But the question is who the hell would handle it? Any ideas on that?

DEAN: Well, I think that is something that Mitchell ought to be charged with.

NIXON: I would think so, too. . . . Your major guy to keep under control is Hunt?

DEAN: That is right.

NIXON: Does he know a lot?

DEAN: He knows so much. . . .

NIXON: Just looking at the immediate problem, don't you think you have to handle Hunt's financial situation damn soon? It seems to me we have to keep the cap on the bottle that much or we don't have any options.

DEAN: That's right.

NIXON: Either that or it all blows right now?

DEAN: That's the question.

Although he had been reluctant to continue the payoffs when he arrived for the meeting, Dean now found himself going along with the president's reasoning. Throughout the conversation, Nixon kept returning to the urgent need to resolve the immediate crisis by paying Hunt the money. "Well, for Christ's sake, get it [the money]," Nixon ordered.

After leaving the Oval Office, Dean telephoned Fred LaRue and informed him of Hunt's latest financial demands. LaRue was taken aback by the amount Hunt was seeking, which was much higher than any past hush-money payment. He said he would need approval from some higher authority before paying the money.

191

Dean referred him to John Mitchell, who told him to meet Hunt's demands.

The only money immediately available was the remainder of the secret fund formerly kept by H. R. Haldeman. But since that fund had dwindled to $278,000, LaRue decided not to pay Hunt the entire $132,000. Instead, he would give him $75,000. He had the money delivered to Hunt through his attorney, William Bittman. The $75,000 delivery brought to $429,500 the total of hush-money payments to the Watergate defendants. Although Hunt was incensed at receiving only partial payment, he made no new threat to expose the cover-up. The day after the payment was made, Mitchell met at the White House with Dean, Haldeman, and John Ehrlichman. He told them that Hunt was "not a problem any more."

But James McCord *was* still very much a problem— and it could not be solved with further hush money. In preparation for sentencing the Watergate defendants, Judge Sirica had ordered federal probation officers to prepare the customary background reports on the seven men. He had told the probation officers to question the defendants about the "motivation, intent, and mitigating circumstances" involved in their participation in the Watergate affair. The six other defendants either refused to respond to the questions or provided answers that gave virtually no new information. McCord, however, decided to use the occasion to begin blowing the lid off the cover-up.

He wrote a long letter to Judge Sirica that contained general references to some elements of the cover-up. The letter said, in part:

Several members of my family have expressed fear for my life if I disclose knowledge of the facts in this matter, either publicly or to any government representative. Whereas I do not share their concerns to the same degree, nevertheless I do believe that retaliatory measures will be taken against me, my family and my friends should I disclose such facts. Such retaliation could destroy careers, income and reputations of persons who are innocent of any guilt whatever.

. . . I will state the following to you, which I hope may be of help to you in meting out justice in this case:

There was political pressure applied to the defendants to plead guilty and remain silent.

Perjury occurred during the trial in matters highly material to the very structure, orientation and impact of the government's case, and to the motivation and intent of the defendants.

Others involved in the Watergate operation were not identified during the trial, when they could have been by those testifying.

The Watergate operation was not a CIA operation. The Cubans may have been misled by others into believing that it was a CIA operation. I know for a fact that it was not. . . .

My motivations were different than those of the others involved, but were not limited to or simply those offered in my defense during the trial. This is no fault of my attorneys, but of the circumstances under which we had to prepare my defense.

Following sentence, I would appreciate the opportunity to talk with you privately in chambers. Since I cannot feel confident in talking with . . . [any] other government representatives, such a discussion with you would be of assistance to me.

I have not discussed the above with my attorneys as a matter of protection for them.

I give this statement freely and voluntarily. . . . The statements are true and correct to the best of my knowledge and belief.

Three days before the scheduled sentencing, McCord took the letter—in a sealed envelope—to Sirica's office and tried to deliver it to the judge. But the court clerk explained that Sirica maintained a policy of refusing to accept correspondence from defendants (apparently to guard against bribery attempts). The clerk suggested that McCord give the envelope to his probation officer, James Morgan. He did so, and Morgan passed the letter on to the judge.

On March 23, when the defendants appeared for sentencing, Sirica opened the proceedings by saying that he had a "preliminary matter" he wanted to get out of the way. He then surprised almost everyone in the courtroom by reading McCord's letter aloud. Sirica said he planned to meet privately with McCord, as requested, and postponed his sentencing in the meantime.

As for the other defendants, the judge dispensed stiff but "provisional" prison sentences to five of them, giving Hunt thirty-five years and Bernard Barker, Frank Sturgis, Virgilio Gonzalez, and Eugenio Martinez forty years each. Under the "provisional" nature of the terms, Sirica said he would review the sentences three months later and might reduce them substantially if the defendants cooperated in investigations by the Senate Watergate Committee and a grand jury. "You must understand that I hold out no promise or hopes of any kind," the judge told the defendants. "But I do say that, should you decide to speak freely, I would have to weigh that factor in appraising what sentence will be finally imposed in each case."

In the case of G. Gordon Liddy, Sirica did not make the sentence provisional. Since Liddy had been the leader of the group and had been the most adamant in insisting he would never cooperate with investigators, the judge decided to make an example of him. He sentenced Liddy to a minimum of six years and eight months and a maximum of twenty years in prison.

(Ultimately, Sirica imposed a one-to-five-year term on McCord. He reduced Hunt's sentence to thirty months to eight years, Barker's to eighteen months to six years, and those of Sturgis, Martinez, and Gonzalez to one to four years.)

Shortly after Judge Sirica read McCord's letter in court, McCord was interviewed privately by the chief counsel to the Watergate committee, Samuel Dash. Among other things, McCord told Dash that John Mitchell had approved the Watergate operation and that John Dean and Jeb Magruder had also had advance knowledge of the bugging activities. Word of the revelations soon found its way into the news media. It quickly became apparent that the Watergate cover-up was beginning to unravel.

McCord's letter and the disclosure that he was cooperating with the Watergate committee helped touch

195

off a scramble by some White House and CREEP officials to protect their own legal positions—even if it
meant abandoning the cover-up. Although they had
previously been bound together by loyalty to the president and his administration, they now began adopting
an attitude of every man for himself. John Dean was
among the first to set off on his own course.

Dean had long harbored misgivings about the cover-
up. When he had expressed some of his doubts to the
president, Nixon had seemed to ignore the warning.
Indeed, in the days that followed, he had tried to draw
Dean even deeper into the cover-up.

In an attempt to counter the Senate committee investigation—even before the McCord revelations—the
president proposed issuing a new public statement denying that he or his aides had been involved in any wrongdoing. He urged Dean to write a report on the Watergate case that could be cited in the statement. The
president said Dean could make self-serving statements
in the report and could claim he had never heard any
discussions of wiretapping or bugging among White
House officials.

Dean did not want to write such a report. For one
thing, he felt it would involve him more seriously than
ever in the cover-up. For another, he feared that Nixon,
Haldeman, and Ehrlichman might try to make him a
scapegoat in the Watergate affair and that the report
would play directly into their hands. If the cover-up
ever fell completely apart, Nixon could accuse Dean of
misleading him with the report. He could say he had
relied on Dean to give him an accurate assessment of

the Watergate situation and that Dean's failure to do so should not be blamed on the president.

Accordingly, Dean stalled on preparing the report. Nixon and Haldeman repeatedly pressured him to get it done. Finally, Nixon suggested he escape the everyday interruptions at his office and work on the report at Camp David, the presidential vacation retreat in the Catoctin Mountains near Thurmont, Maryland. Feeling he could no longer delay it, Dean went to Camp David with his wife, Maureen.

During the five days he spent there, Dean agonized over the situation confronting him. Increasingly, he felt trapped by circumstances that he could not control. He tried several times to write the report, but made little progress. He was convinced that Ehrlichman would never admit his involvement and assumed that Haldeman would continue to protect the president. He later said:

> The more I thought about it, the more I realized that I should step forward because there was no way the situation was going to get better—rather, it would only get worse. My most difficult problem was how I could end this mess without mortally wounding the President.

By that time, largely because of McCord's disclosures, federal prosecutors were showing renewed interest in the Watergate affair. They had called back into session the grand jury that had originally investigated the case. Dean ultimately decided to go to the prosecutors and tell them what he knew about the cover-up.

It must be noted that his motives were not entirely unselfish; he hoped to gain immunity from prosecution or, at least, some form of leniency in return for his cooperation.

On March 28 Haldeman instructed Dean to return to Washington for a White House meeting with John Mitchell and Jeb Magruder. He went back without completing his report. When he met with Mitchell and Magruder, he discovered they wanted assurances that he would tell a false story if questioned by the Watergate committee or the grand jury about the meetings the men had attended with Gordon Liddy. They wanted him to claim that the meetings had concerned only campaign finance laws—not the Liddy political-intelligence plans that led to the Watergate affair. But Dean hedged, saying there was no certainty he would be called to testify. He declined to give them a flat promise that he would tell the false story if he did testify.

Two days later, Nixon turned over to Ehrlichman the responsibility for overseeing White House efforts to bottle up the Watergate scandal. The ostensible reason was Dean's failure to deliver the desired report. That same day, Dean retained a prominent criminal lawyer, Charles Shaffer, to represent him in any legal matters arising out of the Watergate affair. Shaffer began negotiating with federal prosecutors for immunity or leniency in return for Dean's cooperation.

At first, Dean did not tell his White House superiors about the discussions. But on April 8, just before he began to unburden his story of the cover-up to the prosecutors, Dean telephoned Haldeman and reported what he was going to do. Haldeman told him: "I think

198

you ought to think about it because, once the tooth-paste is out of the tube, it's hard to get it back in." Dean had already thought about it, however, and decided to go through with the plan.

Shortly, others also began letting "the toothpaste out of the tube." Once he learned Dean was cooperating with the government lawyers, Magruder realized that his role in the Watergate affair was bound to be exposed. He decided to try to make his own deal with the prose-cutors. After several days of negotiations, he began giving them his versions of the events. Meanwhile, several lesser figures in the case agreed to cooperate in the renewed investigation.

(Dean and Magruder eventually pleaded guilty to limited charges of obstruction of justice and defrauding the United States. Dean was sentenced to one to four years in prison but was released after serving only four months. Magruder was sentenced to ten months to four years but was released after serving seven months.)

When Dean and Magruder began cooperating with the prosecutors, Nixon, Haldeman, and Ehrlichman tried desperately to devise a new strategy for contain-ing the disclosures. Ehrlichman and Haldeman pro-posed that an attempt be made to persuade John Mitchell to step forward and accept the blame for Watergate and the cover-up. Their theory was that Mitchell was such a "big fish"—as former attorney general and head of Nixon's re-election campaign—that his confession and prosecution would fully satisfy the prosecutors and the public. Thus, they reasoned, the investigation could be headed off before it widened to include top White House officials and the president himself. Although reluctant to abandon his old friend and one-time law partner, Nixon ultimately agreed.

When Ehrlichman met with Mitchell to explain the plan, the former attorney general flatly refused to go along with it. He denied being responsible for Watergate and refused to accept the blame. He said it was the White House, not CREEP, that had initiated the plan to have Liddy collect political intelligence. The meeting ended a short time later without the results the president wanted.

Nixon met again with Haldeman and Ehrlichman, and they agreed on still another strategy. Since the cover-up was coming unglued, they would now take steps to make it appear that they were the ones responsible for bringing the facts to light. It was decided that Ehrlichman should give a status report to Attorney General Richard Kleindienst so that the White House could later claim it had taken the initiative in investigating the cover-up. Ehrlichman telephoned Kleindienst and told him:

> The President has had me trying to gather together, as you know, a certain amount of law and facts to be in a position . . . to advise him on the White House involvement . . . in this whole transaction. . . . One of the things I told him was that I had encountered people who appeared to be reticent to come forward because they felt that the presidency was served by their not coming forward. So he had me today . . . straighten them around on that point. . . . My purpose and intent was to advise you of this when I got finished with

the process and tender this information for whatever purposes it would serve.

He also said there were indications that Mitchell and Magruder were "principals" in the Watergate affair and that Dean and LaRue, among others, were deeply implicated in the cover-up. Although such information was already available to some of Kleindienst's subordinates in the Justice Department—since the federal prosecutors worked for the department—it had not yet been passed along through channels to the attorney general. But that situation was remedied within hours.

Kleindienst received a late-night telephone call at home from Assistant Attorney General Henry Petersen, who arranged to visit him immediately with the prosecutors. When his aides arrived, they spent more than three hours relaying the information obtained from Dean and Magruder. Some of those implicated were close friends of the attorney general. Tears slid from his eyes as he heard the details of the allegations against them.

The next day, April 15, Kleindienst went to the White House to discuss the situation with Nixon. He emphasized that the president's two chief aides, Haldeman and Ehrlichman, might face prosecution. He suggested that Nixon ask them to resign or take leaves of absence until the questions about their legal predicaments could be resolved. But the president persuaded him that such a request would amount to finding them guilty "before they have a chance to prove their innocence."

When Kleindienst expressed sorrow and anxiety over the spreading scandal, Nixon told him: "We've just got to ride it through, Dick. . . . The main thing is to handle it right." Kleindienst said he felt the best way "to handle it right" was for him to disqualify himself from overseeing the remainder of the investigation, in view of his close relationships with some of the men who might become defendants. They agreed that Assistant Attorney General Petersen would substitute in the future in supervising the investigation.

Later that day, Kleindienst returned to the White House with Petersen for a second meeting with the president. Petersen reviewed in greater detail the incriminating information against Haldeman and Ehrlichman and urged Nixon to fire them, saying, "these people are going to be a source of vast embarrassment to the presidency." But Nixon reiterated that they should be given a chance to defend themselves. In contrast, he sharply attacked John Dean, saying that Dean was trying to save himself by shifting the blame to Haldeman and Ehrlichman. He suggested that perhaps he should force Dean to resign. Petersen, however, strongly opposed the idea: "Now, here is the first man who has come in to cooperate with us, and certainly we don't want to give the impression that he is being subjected to reprisal because of his cooperation." He urged Nixon to meet with Dean and hear firsthand the allegations he was making to the prosecutors. Nixon agreed.

He met with Dean only a few hours after Kleindienst and Petersen had left his office. Both men seemed plainly uncomfortable. The president cautioned Dean that he should not discuss any of their conversations with the prosecutors. He urged Dean to testify that "the President's action" was responsible for exposing the cover-up and continued pressing him, saying that it was essential the public get the impression the White House was prompting the exposure. Dean, however, declined to go along with a further distortion of the facts.

The next day, Nixon again summoned Dean to his office. This time, in spite of Petersen's previous advice, the president tried to force Dean's resignation. He handed Dean two typed letters and asked him to sign both of them. In the first letter, Dean would be requesting a leave of absence "in view of my increasing involvement in the Watergate matter, my impending appearance before the grand jury and the probability of its action." In the second, Dean would be resigning "as a result of my involvement in the Watergate matter." Nixon said he would not immediately make public either letter. Instead, he would hold both of them and, if he later deemed it advisable, would release whichever letter best suited his purpose.

Dean, however, refused to sign either one, saying he would prepare his own. Later in the day, he returned to Nixon's office with a letter that read:

> Dear Mr. President: You informed me that Bob Haldeman and John Ehrlichman have verbally tendered their requests to give them immediate and indefinite leave of absence from the staff. So I declare I wish also to confirm my similar request that I be given such a leave of absence from the staff.

Of course, Haldeman and Ehrlichman had made no such requests. The wording of the letter was a ploy on

203

Dean's part, intended as a warning that he would not allow himself to be used as the scapegoat. The meeting broke up without agreement on what would happen next. Nixon later telephoned Dean and said he would soon make another public statement on Watergate, but that it would include no mention of any resignations.

The president had decided a new statement was necessary to give the impression he was taking the initiative in investigating the cover-up. As he put it in a conversation with Haldeman and Ehrlichman: "We have to get out in front in some way." Thus on April 17 he went before the television cameras and said in part:

> On March twenty-first, as a result of serious charges which came to my attention . . . I began intensive new inquiries into this whole matter. . . . The attorney general, Assistant Attorney General Petersen and I met at length . . . to review the facts which had come to me in my investigation and also to review the progress of the Department of Justice investigation. I can report today that there have been major developments in the case concerning which it would be improper to be more specific now.

In the statement, the president retreated from his previous position on executive privilege and said that White House officials would be permitted to testify, after all, before the Senate Watergate Committee. He also said that any government official indicted by the grand jury would be suspended from his job and, if convicted, fired.

If Nixon believed his statement would ease the pressure on the administration, he was mistaken. Suspicion of the White House continued to mount. Nixon received word that Dean was threatening to implicate him personally in the cover-up. This threat was heightened when Dean's attorney, Charles Shaffer, told reporters that if Dean did not receive immunity from prosecution, "we are going to try Ehrlichman, Haldeman, Nixon and this whole administration." Nixon had been opposing grants of immunity to important government officials—a strategy some felt was aimed at discouraging Dean from cooperating fully with the prosecutors.

Nixon became more adamant than ever about the necessity for forcing Dean out of his White House job—but came to realize that he could not get rid of him unless he simultaneously ousted Haldeman and Ehrlichman. He tried to explain his reasoning to his two long-time aides who, predictably, resisted that approach. As Ehrlichman put it to the president: "If Dean says, 'What about Haldeman and Ehrlichman?' you say, 'John, I'm talking to you about you. Now, I'll take care of them my own way. I'm not going to have you bargaining with me.' "

Reaching a decision on the matter was a painful process, but Nixon was under increasing pressure to remove Haldeman and Ehrlichman before they further weakened his position. Among those most persistently urging such action was Henry Petersen. "I think they have made you, wittingly or unwittingly, very vulnerable. At least in public forums, they eroded confidence in the office of the presidency."

Nixon tried to soften the blow for Haldeman and

Ehrlichman by offering them a measure of financial stability if they left the White House. He suggested they could go to work for a nonprofit foundation being established in his name to build a library that would house his presidential papers and other documents. He also offered them more than $200,000 in cash, ostensibly to hire lawyers and pay family expenses. But Haldeman and Ehrlichman declined the offers, apparently fearing these might be interpreted as still more hush-money payments.

Finally, however, they grudgingly agreed to resign. Meanwhile, Attorney General Kleindienst decided that he would also resign—chiefly because his close association with some of those emerging as central figures in the cover-up would represent a continuing embarrassment to the president. Nixon decided to appoint Defense Secretary Elliot Richardson to replace Kleindienst.

The resignations of Kleindienst, Haldeman, Ehrlichman, and Dean—and the appointment of Richardson—were announced on April 30. That night, the president made another televised address in which he described the decisions to reshuffle his administration.

He strongly defended Haldeman, Ehrlichman, and Kleindienst in the speech. Describing Haldeman and Ehrlichman as "two of the finest public servants it has ever been my privilege to know," he said the decision to accept their resignations was one of the most difficult he had ever made. He said the resignations involved "no implication whatever of personal wrongdoing on their part." As for Kleindienst, the President said he had "no personal involvement" in the Watergate affair. Pointedly, however, Nixon refrained from expressing regret

206

about the resignation of Dean. Nor did he make any statement vouching for Dean's integrity or clearing him of wrongdoing in the scandal.

The address also contained passages in which Nixon accepted responsibility—in a backhanded way—for allowing Watergate to happen. He said he had made a conscious decision in 1972 to concentrate on his duties as president and thus had left the management of his re-election campaign to others:

> The easiest course would be for me to blame those to whom I delegated the responsibility to run the campaign. But that would be a cowardly thing to do. I will not place the blame on subordinates —on people whose zeal exceeded their judgment and who may have done wrong in a cause they deeply believed to be right. In any organization, the man at the top must bear the responsibility. That responsibility, therefore, belongs here in this office. I accept that.

Nixon pledged he would do everything possible to see that those responsible for Watergate and the cover-up were punished. He said he was giving Elliot Richardson "absolute authority to make all decisions bearing upon the prosecution of the Watergate case and related matters." That authority, Nixon said, included the power—if Richardson saw fit—to name a special prosecutor from outside the Justice Department to handle the case.

Like all cabinet appointments, Richardson's appointment as attorney general was subject to confirmation by the Senate. During the confirmation hearings, Richardson tried to demonstrate his independence to the senators by disclosing that he would name as special Watergate prosecutor a highly respected Harvard Law School professor, Archibald Cox, a Democrat who had held a top Justice Department position in President John F. Kennedy's administration. Cox, for his part, said he did not intend "to be intimidated by anybody." The Senate approved Richardson's appointment.

In mid-May, the Senate Watergate Committee launched its televised hearings into the scandal. While a fascinated public watched hour after hour of proceedings, such witnesses as James McCord, Jeb Magruder, and John Dean described in rich detail the events surrounding the Watergate bugging and the cover-up. Among those Magruder implicated were Mitchell, Haldeman, Ehrlichman, Dean, Charles Colson, Fred LaRue, and himself. Dean went an important step beyond that—implicating Nixon in the cover-up.

Nixon and his defenders argued that much of the testimony was self-serving, that it was uncorroborated by documentary evidence and amounted to the word of the witnesses against that of others. But then an event occurred that provided a possible means of obtaining the necessary proof.

On July 13 members of the Watergate committee staff were privately interviewing Alexander Butterfield, a former White House aide. Butterfield, who had become administrator of the Federal Aviation Administration, had previously served as deputy assistant to the president. In that capacity, he had overseen many of the "housekeeping" functions at the White House, with responsibility for ensuring the smooth running of the president's official day, the maintenance of records, and liaison with security agencies such as the Secret Service.

Questioning Butterfield were Eugene Boyce, an assistant majority counsel of the Watergate committee; Donald Sanders, deputy minority counsel; and Scott Armstrong, a committee investigator. For several hours, the interview concerned routine matters relating to the way Nixon ran his office. During all that time, a nagging question had been sticking at the backs of the committee staffers' minds. John Dean had testified before the committee that, toward the end of his tenure as Nixon's counsel, he came to suspect that the president was secretly tape-recording their conversations. Later, the White House had provided the committee with written summaries of Nixon's discussions with Dean. The summaries were so detailed that they gave some the impression they might have been prepared with the help of such recordings.

Finally, Sanders asked Butterfield the crucial question: "Do you know of any basis for the implication in Dean's testimony that conversations in the President's office are recorded?"

Butterfield paused for a moment. "I was hoping you fellows wouldn't ask me about that. . . . Well, yes, there's a recording system in the President's office."

He explained that Nixon had ordered a secret taping system installed in February 1971, supposedly to preserve conversations for "historical purposes." The Secret Service, acting on instructions, had placed hidden microphones not only in the Oval Office but also in several other rooms where the president worked in the

209

White House and at the presidential lodge at Camp David. In addition, recording devices had been placed on telephones regularly used by Nixon. Secret Service agents changed the tapes daily and stored them for the president's future use.

The implications of Butterfield's account were staggering. Nixon had obviously betrayed countless administration officials, senators, congressmen, foreign leaders, and others who thought they had been speaking to him in confidence. Even some of his closest advisers had been unaware of the existence of the taping system. Although Butterfield and Haldeman knew about it, Ehrlichman and most other White House officials did not. More important from the standpoint of the investigation was the fact that the secret tapes undoubtedly contained significant clues to responsibility for the Watergate operation and the cover-up. If the tapes could be obtained by the committee and the special prosecutor, they could prove invaluable in checking the truthfulness of testimony by Dean, Magruder, and other witnesses. And there was always the possibility the tapes would provide information unavailable from any other source.

After completing the interview with Butterfield, the committee staffers immediately reported the existence of the tapes to their superiors. Three days later, Butterfield was called as a surprise witness at the televised hearings. His testimony about the tapes created a national sensation. Many Americans, including leading political figures from both major parties, sharply assailed Nixon for having the secret recordings made.

The Watergate committee promptly voted to ask the

president to deliver "all relevant documents and tapes under the control of the White House that relate to the matters the committee is authorized to investigate." Special Prosecutor Cox followed up with a similar request. Nixon waited a week before responding to the requests. During that time, presidential aides disclosed that the taping system had been removed from the White House shortly after Butterfield's testimony because it had become an "embarrassment."

On July 23 Nixon sent letters to Senator Ervin and to Cox saying that he would not provide the requested tapes. His letter to Ervin cited the doctrines of separation of powers and executive privilege as the main reasons for his refusal. The president said he had listened to some of the tapes and that they were "entirely consistent with what I know to be the truth." But he conceded that not everyone might agree with that assessment.

Derisively describing Nixon's response as "a rather remarkable letter," Ervin read it aloud at a committee hearing. "You will notice the President says he has heard the tapes or some of them and they sustain his position," Ervin said. "But he says he is not going to let anybody else hear them for fear they might draw a different conclusion. In other words, the President says they are susceptible of, as I construe it, two different interpretations—one favorable to his aides and one not favorable to his aides."

The committee set the stage for an important legal confrontation with the president by voting unanimously to subpoena five tapes of conversations between Nixon and Dean. Ervin said he deeply regretted that it had become necessary to take such action. "I have very different ideas of separation of powers from those expressed by the President. . . . I am certain that the doctrine of separation of powers does not impose upon any President either the duty or the power to undertake to separate a congressional committee from access to the truth concerning alleged criminal activities. . . ."

Later that day, Special Prosecutor Cox subpoenaed nine tapes of White House conversations. His subpoena and the one issued by the Senate committee were served on Nixon's White House lawyers. Three days later, the president announced he would not comply.

Cox and the Watergate committee quickly filed lawsuits in Judge John Sirica's court asking that Nixon be ordered to turn over the tapes. Sirica gave priority to Cox's suit. One reason was that Cox's criminal investigation was considered more urgent than the Senate committee's inquiry, aimed at proposing remedial legislation to close legal loopholes exposed in the Watergate affair. Another was that Cox's suit did not involve the thorny constitutional issue of separation of powers. Since Cox's office was a part of the executive branch of government —theoretically subject to supervision by the president— the separation-of-powers argument did not apply.

Nixon's lawyers filed a brief with the court arguing that executive privilege protected the president from being forced to surrender the tapes: "If the special prosecutor should be successful in the attempt to compel disclosure of recordings of presidential conversations, the damage to the institution of the presidency will be severe and irreparable."

Cox answered with a brief contending that the grand

jury investigating the Watergate affair was entitled to all available evidence. "There is no exception for the President from the guiding principle that the public, in pursuit of justice, has a right to every man's evidence."

After hearing oral arguments from the opposing lawyers, Judge Sirica ruled basically in favor of Cox on August 29. "The court fails to perceive any reason for suspending the power of the courts to get evidence . . . simply because it is the President of the United States who holds the evidence," Sirica's decision said. It stopped short, however, of ordering Nixon to give the tapes directly to Cox or the grand jury. Instead, it directed the president to deliver them to Sirica. The judge would listen to the tapes privately and determine whether any portions were subject to legitimate claims of executive privilege. After eliminating any privileged sections, the decision said, Sirica would give the remainder of the tapes to the grand jury.

The White House announced that Nixon's lawyers would appeal the decision but did not guarantee that the president would comply with the ruling if he lost the appeal. In advance of Sirica's decision, the president had said he would obey a "definitive ruling" on the matter by the Supreme Court. He had not said, however, what he would consider "definitive." Cox also announced that he would appeal Sirica's ruling and seek to have the president ordered to give the tapes directly to the grand jury.

Before the appeal could reach the Supreme Court, it first had to be considered by the U.S. Court of Appeals for the District of Columbia. On September 11,

213

the appeals court heard arguments on the case from Cox and one of the president's attorneys.

In an effort to avoid a possible constitutional crisis on the issue, the seven appeals court judges unanimously recommended that Nixon and Cox try to reach a compromise. They suggested that Nixon voluntarily turn over selected portions of the tapes to his own lawyers and Cox, who would then decide collectively which sections of the conversations should be given to the grand jury. Cox met several times with the presidential attorneys in an attempt to work out such a settlement, but they were never able to reach agreement. The opposing lawyers reported to the court that no compromise seemed possible.

Thus the judges were obliged to resume pondering the appeal. Meanwhile, Cox and Nixon were engaged in disputes on issues other than the tapes. Cox had asked the president and his aides to surrender numerous documents bearing on the investigation. In some cases, Nixon had flatly refused to comply; in others, he had stalled for interminable periods in responding to the requests. Cox was growing increasingly insistent. In one letter to the president's lawyers, he said that the repeated delays were hampering his investigation.

For his part, Nixon grew ever more disenchanted with the special prosecutor. He apparently feared Cox's investigation would reveal his own role in the cover-up. The president had harbored reservations from the outset about the wisdom of establishing a special prosecutor's office. Now, he and some of his aides began discussing the possibility of getting rid of Cox.

On October 12 the appeals court upheld Sirica's

214

original decision and ordered Nixon to turn the tapes over to him. A week's delay was ordered before the decision would take effect.

During that time, Nixon decided to try another plan that called for Richardson to fire Cox. Since the special prosecutor's office would then be vacant, the subpoena for the tapes and the resulting court case would become academic. The president would then give Judge Sirica summaries of the conversations on the tapes—but not the tapes themselves.

Richardson bridled at the proposal. He said he had pledged during his Senate confirmation hearings that Cox would not be fired except for "extraordinary improprieties." Cox had committed no such improprieties, Richardson said, and thus he could not fire him. He threatened to resign as attorney general if Nixon insisted on Cox's removal.

A short time later, Alexander Haig—an army general who had replaced H. R. Haldeman as Nixon's chief aide—proposed an alternate plan for averting enforcement of the court order. He suggested that an independent third party, conservative Democratic Senator John Stennis of Mississippi, listen to the tapes and prepare transcripts of the sections relevant to the investigation. The transcripts would then be turned over to Cox and the grand jury. Richardson said the idea was worthy of consideration.

After conferring with the president, Haig called Richardson back and said Nixon had approved the new plan but had attached several conditions. Cox would have to agree that, if he received the transcripts to be prepared by Stennis, he would ask for no more White House tapes or documents. And if Cox would not accept those terms, Richardson would have to fire him.

Richardson said that he would try to persuade Cox to accept the plan, but that he would not fire him if he refused. After reading Richardson's memorandum, Cox replied in writing that the principle of having a third party prepare transcripts of the tapes was "not unacceptable" to him. He said that he was willing to try to work out a solution that would prevent any "avoidable confrontation with the President," but that he had almost a dozen objections to the proposed plan. For one thing, he wanted to include a section clearly establishing that he would have the right to obtain additional evidence from the White House, if necessary, even after he got the transcripts. For another, he wanted Nixon to guarantee that, if the courts were dissatisfied with partial transcripts, the White House would provide the full tapes.

Richardson met with Haig and the White House lawyers to discuss Cox's response. Haig and the lawyers regarded the response as a flat rejection of the plan and wanted Cox fired, but Richardson again resisted that idea. It was decided that presidential attorney Charles Alan Wright should make one last effort to work out a compromise with Cox. But if that attempt failed, the White House men insisted, Cox would have to be dismissed.

The discussions between Wright and Cox proved fruitless, as were still further attempts to reach a compromise. Finally, on October 19 (the deadline for Nixon's lawyers to file an appeal with the Supreme Court), the president sent Richardson a letter directing

216

him to order Cox "to make no further attempts by judicial process to obtain tapes, notes or memoranda of Presidential conversations." Richardson read the letter over the telephone to Cox but emphasized that he was not ordering the special prosecutor to comply with Nixon's instructions—merely informing him of the letter's contents.

Later that day, Nixon issued a public statement revealing the action he had taken "to bring the issue of the Watergate tapes to an end." Nixon announced his intention to go through with the plan to have Senator Stennis prepare transcripts of the tapes, even though no agreement had been reached with Cox on the matter.

Cox promptly issued a statement of his own, refusing to obey the president's order. The next day, Saturday, October 20, he called a press conference to explain his decision:

> I am certainly not out to "get" the President of the United States. . . . I think it is my duty as special prosecutor, as an officer of the court and as the representative of the grand jury to bring to the court's attention what seems to me to be noncompliance with the court's order. If the court should rule that there was satisfactory compliance, then it would be my duty in those same capacities to abide by the court's order. . . .

After hearing what Cox had said, Nixon decided once and for all that the special prosecutor had to go. On his instructions, Haig called Richardson and ordered him

217

to fire Cox. "I can't do that," the attorney general insisted. "I guess I'd better come over and resign."

Before going to the White House, Richardson conferred with two of his top aides, Deputy Attorney General William Ruckelshaus and Solicitor General Robert Bork. He asked Ruckelshaus, who was next in line to run the Justice Department once the attorney general resigned, what he would do if Nixon ordered him to dismiss Cox. Ruckelshaus said he would follow Richardson's lead and resign. Richardson then put the same question to Bork. The solicitor general, who had never thought the special prosecutor's office was necessary, replied that he would abide by an instruction from Nixon to fire Cox. "Somebody has to carry out the President's order," Bork said.

When he reached the White House, Richardson was ushered into a meeting with Nixon and Haig. He told them he was submitting his resignation. Nixon asked him to delay quitting—to fire Cox, wait at least a week, and then resign. Richardson refused, and the president testily accused him of putting a "purely personal commitment" before the national interest.

"I'm acting on the basis of national interest, as I see it," Richardson retorted.

"Your perception of national interest is so different from mine," Nixon replied.

After Richardson left the White House, Haig telephoned Deputy Attorney General Ruckelshaus and relayed instructions from Nixon to fire Cox. Ruckelshaus refused. "Your commander in chief has given you an order," Haig said. "You have no alternative."

218

"Other than to resign," Ruckelshaus replied. He told Haig, however, that Bork apparently had no objection to firing Cox. Haig telephoned Bork a few minutes later and summoned him to the White House. There, Bork was named acting attorney general. He immediately wrote a brief letter firing the special prosecutor and had it hand-delivered to Cox.

Later, Presidential Press Secretary Ronald Ziegler called reporters to an unusual Saturday night news briefing. He announced that Richardson and Ruckelshaus had resigned, that Bork had been designated as acting attorney general and that Bork had fired Cox. Moreover, he said the office of special prosecutor had been abolished.

The developments described by Ziegler quickly became known as the Saturday Night Massacre. And they touched off a vast, explosive outpouring of indignation from public officials, political leaders, and the American people. Citizens in all sections of the country began telephoning, writing, and cabling their protests to Washington. Many called on Nixon to resign, as did the leaders of organized labor and some members of Congress. In the House of Representatives, many Democratic members started drawing up resolutions calling for the president's impeachment. The resolutions were quickly referred to the House Judiciary Committee for consideration.

Even some Republican congressmen and senators bitterly attacked Nixon for failing to deal forthrightly with the Watergate scandal and cover-up. Influential House Republicans warned that they would find it difficult to fight the proposed impeachment proceedings unless Nixon surrendered the subpoenaed tape recordings.

The president was taken aback by the scope of the antagonism the Saturday Night Massacre had unleashed. He quickly recognized that he had seriously misjudged the national mood. After conferring with his leading advisers, he decided he would have to do something dramatic to demonstrate that he was not pursuing a course of absolute defiance of the courts and the public will.

An opportunity for such a demonstration arose three days later, on October 23. Presidential lawyer Charles Alan Wright was scheduled to appear before Judge Sirica to give Nixon's formal response to the court order directing surrender of the tapes. He originally planned to present the proposal that Senator Stennis provide a partial transcript of the tapes. But at the eleventh hour, Nixon ordered that plan abandoned.

Instead, when Wright stood before Judge Sirica, he announced that the president would "comply in all respects" with the court order. The statement caught everyone, including Sirica, by surprise. Sirica, in fact, asked whether he understood correctly—that the tapes "will be delivered to this court?"

"To the court," Wright confirmed. Then he added: "This President does not defy the law." He said, however, that it would take a little time for White House officials to gather the tapes and index them, as specified in the court orders.

Thus Nixon had done a complete about-face. Three days after that, the president made another strategic turnabout. He announced he had changed his mind about abolishing the special prosecutor's office. Acting

Attorney General Bork would shortly name a new special prosecutor to take Cox's place; he promised "total cooperation" with the new prosecutor.

Eventually chosen as Cox's successor was attorney Leon Jaworski of Houston, Texas. A pillar of the legal establishment, Jaworski was a former president of the American Bar Association. He was a Democrat and had been a long-time confidant of the late President Lyndon B. Johnson. Nixon obviously hoped the appointment of a man of Jaworski's standing would help restore at least a bit of the White House's sagging credibility on Watergate. Jaworski was initially reluctant to take the job, but Alexander Haig appealed to him on the ground that it was his patriotic duty to accept. Haig assured Jaworski that he would have the right to file suit to obtain any evidence he felt he needed from the White House. And he pledged that the new special prosecutor would not be fired without the agreement of the Republican and Democratic leaders of both houses of Congress. Jaworski ultimately was persuaded to take the position.

Nixon anticipated that, in view of the circumstances under which his last two attorneys general had left office, he might encounter trouble in getting the Senate to confirm the appointment of a new attorney general. At least in part to deal with that problem, he decided to nominate a senator—Republican William Saxbe of Ohio—for the job. In keeping with tradition, many senators were more amenable to the appointment of one of their colleagues than they might have been to that of an outsider. Once the Senate had approved Saxbe's nomination and he had been sworn in as attorney general, Robert Bork returned to his former job as solicitor general.

Meanwhile, serious new problems arose for the president concerning his credibility on Watergate. On October 31 his attorneys belatedly reported to Judge Sirica and members of the special prosecutor's staff that two of the nine tapes over which the court battle had been fought actually did not exist. Both tapes had been considered essential to the special prosecutor in trying to assess blame for the cover-up. One involved a telephone conversation between Nixon and John Mitchell on June 20, 1972, just three days after the Watergate arrests. The other concerned a meeting between Nixon and John Dean on April 15, 1973, shortly after Dean began cooperating with federal prosecutors.

The discussion between Nixon and Mitchell had been their first since the arrests. Thus a tape of the conversation—if it existed—presumably could have provided important clues on how much each of them knew about the Watergate affair. As for the meeting between Dean and Nixon, Dean had testified before the Senate Watergate Committee that the discussion had included such subjects as the hush-money payments to the Watergate defendants and possible executive clemency for E. Howard Hunt. A tape could have proved or disproved Dean's account.

Although the disclosure that the tapes were missing was initially made in private, Sirica quickly focused the public spotlight on the matter by convening a court hearing to try to determine why the recordings did not exist.

Judge Sirica's hearing never solved the mystery of the

missing tapes, but many Americans were left with the suspicion that Nixon or his aides had destroyed the recordings because they contained damaging evidence. This suspicion was heightened when the White House conceded that the president had known the tapes were missing a full month before his lawyers reported the problem to Sirica.

The further erosion of confidence in the president produced a spate of demands for his resignation. They came not only from leading political figures in both parties, but also from such influential publications as the *New York Times* and *Time* magazine. Nixon responded with a televised speech in which he vowed: "I have no intention whatever of walking away from the job I was elected to do."

In an attempt to recapture the initiative, Nixon launched an ambitious public relations campaign in which he courted support from politicians and the public. He invited almost 300 members of the House and Senate—mostly Republicans—to the White House for a series of meetings where he defended his record on Watergate. And he embarked on an extensive public-speaking tour in which he urged the nation to "put Watergate behind us." In one appearance, before a convention of newspaper editors, Nixon said: "People have the right to know whether or not their President is a crook. Well, I am not a crook."

The public relations offensive appeared to be having at least partial success for a time, but then Nixon was again thrown back on the defensive by a startling new development. On November 21 White House lawyer Buzhardt reported to Judge Sirica that there was an eighteen-minute gap on one of the seven remaining tapes Nixon had been ordered to turn over to the court. A loud buzzing noise—but no conversation—could be heard during the eighteen-minute period on a tape of a meeting between Nixon and H. R. Haldeman three days after the Watergate arrests.

Sirica convened new hearings to try to determine the cause of the gap. The hearings produced fresh suspicion of Nixon and his staff. There was evidence that the meeting between Nixon and Haldeman had lasted an hour and a quarter and that the men had discussed various subjects, including Watergate. The buzzing on the tape eliminated all the conversation about Watergate, but the discussion of every other topic could be plainly heard. Those circumstances seemed too odd to be coincidental.

White House officials produced a theory on how the gap could have occurred. They said Nixon had decided to study the subpoenaed tapes before surrendering them to Sirica and had asked his secretary, Rose Mary Woods, to prepare typewritten transcripts of the conversations. Miss Woods testified at the hearings that, while she was listening to the Nixon-Haldeman tape and transcribing it, she was interrupted by a telephone call. She said she reached for the "stop" button on the tape recorder she was using but may have accidentally hit the "record" button instead as she simultaneously answered the telephone. Pushing the "record" button would have erased the tape. Miss Woods said her telephone call lasted no longer than five minutes. When she resumed listening to the tape, she said, she heard the buzzing noise.

224

Even if her account were accepted, it left several important unanswered questions. Why should the gap have been eighteen minutes long if her telephone call had lasted only five minutes? What had caused the buzzing noise, which could not be explained by the mere pushing of the "record" button? And how did it happen that the gap covered only the period during which Watergate had been discussed?

Sirica appointed six experts on recording equipment to study the tape and try to solve the mystery. After conducting scientific tests, the experts reported that the gap had resulted from at least five distinct erasures, each requiring separate pushes on the buttons of the recording machine. They ruled out the possibility that one accidental push of a button—such as Miss Woods had described—could have been responsible. Although the experts did not flatly charge that the tape had been deliberately erased, they said the evidence they found was consistent with intentional erasure.

At Sirica's request, a grand jury investigated the tape gap to try to determine whether any criminal wrongdoing was involved. The investigation determined that only five people—Nixon, Miss Woods, and three presidential aides—apparently had opportunities to erase the tape. But the grand jury never returned any indictment concerning the matter.

Nixon eventually surrendered the seven existing subpoenaed tapes to Sirica. The judge ruled that three of the tapes were subject to claims of executive privilege and should not be turned over to Special Prosecutor Jaworski. He delivered the other four to Jaworski, who presented them along with a mass of other evidence to the grand jury investigating the Watergate cover-up.

Ultimately, the grand jury indicted seven men on charges of conspiracy, obstruction of justice, and perjury in the cover-up case. The defendants were John Mitchell, H. R. Haldeman, John Ehrlichman, former White House aides Charles Colson and Gordon Strachan, former CREEP official Robert Mardian, and CREEP attorney Kenneth Parkinson.

Mardian and Parkinson were found not guilty at a trial, and the charges against Colson and Strachan were dropped. But Mitchell, Haldeman, and Ehrlichman were found guilty and sentenced to twenty-five months to five years in prison. However, Judge Sirica made them eligible for release after they had served only fractions of that time. He did so only when all three had made written statements apologizing for their criminal acts.

13 THE IMPEACHMENT PROCESS

Soon after the indictment of the seven defendants was announced, it was disclosed that the grand jury had gathered evidence indicating Nixon was seriously enmeshed in the cover-up. The grand jury had considered indicting Nixon but had abandoned the idea when told by Jaworski that the law prohibited indictment of a president while he was in office. A confidential report on Nixon's alleged involvement in the cover-up and a large briefcase filled with corroborating evidence were given to Sirica by the grand jury.

Following the Saturday Night Massacre, the House Judiciary Committee had been plodding along in methodical fashion with the preliminary steps in its impeachment investigation. Committee Chairman Peter Rodino, Jr., a New Jersey Democrat, ordered the hiring of a staff of more than a hundred for the inquiry. Appointed to head the staff as chief counsel was John Doar, a former top official of the Justice Department's Civil Rights Division who had won wide respect for his government service during the Eisenhower, Kennedy, and Johnson administrations.

In order for Nixon to be removed from office, a three-stage process would have to take place. First, the Judiciary Committee would have to draw up and approve one or more articles of impeachment. Second, the House of Representatives would have to vote for impeachment—a process somewhat comparable to the return of an indictment by a grand jury. Third, the Senate would have to conduct a trial and vote for conviction. In the only previous attempt to remove a president by such means, the House had voted in 1868 to impeach President Andrew Johnson but the Senate had failed to convict him.

One of the first major tasks confronting the Judiciary Committee staff involved defining an impeachable offense. The Constitution said the president and other federal officials "shall be removed from office on impeachment for, and conviction of, treason, bribery or other high crimes and misdemeanors." But there was no clear agreement on what constituted "high crimes and misdemeanors." Must they be actual violations of specific criminal laws? Opinions varied.

It was not until late February of 1974 that the committee staff completed a report on the issue. It traced the history of impeachment provisions in England, upon which the American procedures were modeled, and in the United States. In addition to Andrew Johnson, eleven lesser U.S. officials had been impeached over the years, and four of them had been convicted by the Senate. The report contended that an impeachable offense did not necessarily have to be a violation of the criminal law:

The emphasis has been on the significant effects of the conduct—undermining the integrity of office, disregard of constitutional duties and oath of office, arrogation of power, abuse of the governmental process, adverse impact on the system of government. Clearly, these effects can be brought about in ways not anticipated by the criminal law. . . . Impeachment was evolved . . . to cope with both the inadequacy of criminal standards and the impotence of courts to deal with the conduct of great public figures. It would be anomalous if the framers [of the Constitution], having barred criminal sanctions from the impeachment remedy and limited it to removal and possible disqualification from office, intended to restrict the grounds for impeachment to conduct that was criminal.

Nixon's lawyers and some Republican members of the Judiciary Committee predictably disagreed with the conclusions in the staff report. They argued that only actual crimes could be considered impeachable offenses. The issue would continue to be debated throughout the committee's deliberations.

Although the committee was doing some original investigating of its own, it was relying heavily on the

229

use of evidence gathered in the inquiries by the special prosecutor, the grand juries, and the Senate Watergate Committee. The committee asked Judge Sirica for the confidential grand jury report and the briefcase full of evidence on Nixon's involvement in the cover-up. Attorneys for the defendants in the cover-up case filed suit to prevent delivery of the documents, claiming such a release would cause publicity unfair to their clients. Nixon did not join in the suit, apparently to avoid giving the appearance he was trying to prevent embarrassing information from coming to light. Sirica, pointing out that the evidence in question focused on Nixon's conduct and that he had not objected to its release, ruled that the documents should be given to the committee. After an appeals court upheld his decision, the judge handed the evidence over to committee counsel Doar.

The Judiciary Committee, however, encountered considerably more trouble in trying to gather other evidence it wanted. Roadblocks were continually placed in the committee's path by Nixon and his aides. The committee obtained from Jaworski a list of all the documents and tapes provided by the White House to the special prosecutor's office. Doar asked the White House to supply the committee with copies of all the materials given to Jaworski, plus more than forty additional tapes. A newly retained White House lawyer, James St. Clair, replied that the committee could have the materials provided Jaworski but indicated that the additional tapes would not be made available.

The committee continued pressing for delivery of those tapes, arguing that they were essential to the investigation. White House officials stalled for more than a month, declining to give a flat yes or no response to the committee's request. Several deadlines for delivery of the tapes were set by the committee but extended at the urging of St. Clair. Finally, the committee ran out of patience. On April 11 it issued a subpoena demanding that the tapes be surrendered by April 25. Never before had a House committee issued a subpoena to a president.

Nixon found himself caught in a dilemma. On the one hand, he did not want to release the additional tapes because he knew they contained incriminating conversations. On the other hand, adoption of a totally defiant posture could damage his case in the impeachment proceedings. Indeed, some congressmen claimed that refusal to honor the committee subpoena could itself be considered an impeachable offense.

The president finally decided on a ploy designed to make it appear that he was cooperating with the Judiciary Committee although he was actually giving the panel less than it had demanded. Instead of delivering the subpoenaed tapes, Nixon would release to the committee and the public carefully selected and edited partial transcripts of some of the conversations. After obtaining a five-day extension of the effective date of the committee's subpoena, he went on national television on April 29 to announce his decision.

As the television cameras focused on the president, viewers could see nearby a pile of fifty loose-leaf books containing transcripts of the conversations that were being released. The tall stack gave the impression that Nixon was making public an enormous amount of ma-

231

terial. Actually, the books contained an average of little more than two dozen pages each. The president made frequent references during his address to the supposedly broad scope of the transcripts:

> In these folders that you see over here on my left are more than 1,200 pages of transcripts of private conversations I participated in. Everything that is relevant is included—the rough as well as the smooth, the strategy sessions, the exploration of alternatives, the weighing of human and political costs. As far as what the President knew and did with regard to Watergate and the cover-up is concerned, these materials—together with those already made available—will tell it all.

Nixon also said he would invite Chairman Rodino and the ranking Republican on the Judiciary Committee, Congressman Edward Hutchinson of Michigan, to listen to full tapes of the conversations in order to verify the accuracy of the transcripts.

Besides releasing the transcripts, Nixon issued a fifty-page statement summarizing some of the conversations and interpreting them in a fashion most favorable to him. "Throughout the period of the Watergate affair, the raw material of these recorded confidential conversations establishes that the President had no prior knowledge of the break-in and that he had no knowledge of any cover-up prior to March 21, 1973," the statement said.

Despite Nixon's protestations of innocence, many Americans were shocked by the contents of the tran-

232

scripts. And although the president had been prepared for some negative reactions, he was jolted by the depth and breadth of the public outcry. The transcripts showed that Nixon's emphasis throughout the Watergate affair had been on protecting himself and containing the scandal—not on bringing the facts to light. They reflected cynical attitudes and cutthroat policies among the president and his aides. The language was crude, often profane—although some of the worst profanity had been deleted. Even some of Nixon's firmest long-time supporters were outraged. Senate Minority Leader Hugh Scott of Pennsylvania—who had been a stalwart defender of the president—spoke for many of them when he described the contents of the transcripts as "disgusting, shabby, immoral."

Moreover, as Nixon's critics quickly noted, the transcripts fell far short of fulfilling the president's claim that they would "tell it all." To begin with, he had made the selection of which conversations would be included. Beyond that, the transcripts contained numerous gaps. In almost 1,800 cases, the transcripts claimed that the gaps were caused by "unintelligible" or "inaudible" sections of the tape recordings. In still other cases, the White House claimed sections were omitted because they were not "related to presidential action." Many such omissions came at critical points in the conversations, leading to suspicion that damaging remarks had deliberately been deleted.

Further doubt was cast on Nixon's credibility when Judiciary Committee members compared portions of the transcripts with the tapes already in their possession that had previously been released to the special

233

prosecutor. Substantial discrepancies were found between the transcripts and the tapes. Almost invariably, the accounts in the transcripts were more favorable to the president's cause.

The Judiciary Committee quickly decided not to accept the transcripts as substitutes for the tapes it had subpoenaed. As Chairman Rodino put it: "The President has not complied with our subpoena. We did not subpoena an edited White House version. . . ."

Some committee members wanted to cite Nixon for contempt of Congress, but Rodino persuaded them that such an action would be unenforceable against a sitting president. Nobody could seriously expect a judge to send the president to jail for refusal to comply with the subpoena. Instead, the committee voted to send Nixon a letter putting him on formal notice that he had failed to honor the subpoena.

The White House responded with a statement that the president had decided not to surrender any more tapes or other evidence. Undaunted, the committee issued two more subpoenas—one for eleven additional tapes and the other for White House documents. Nixon replied in a letter that he had no intention of honoring the two latest subpoenas or any "further subpoenas as may hereafter be issued." The committee fired back a letter warning that the president's continued refusal to comply "might constitute a ground for impeachment."

Special Prosecutor Jaworski also was faced with increasing resistance from Nixon and his aides, despite the promises of cooperation given him before he took the special prosecutor's job. When he subpoenaed an additional sixty-four presidential tapes, Nixon refused

234

to supply them and sent his lawyers into Judge Sirica's court seeking to have the subpoena invalidated.

White House attorney James St. Clair contended at a hearing conducted by Sirica that, since Jaworski was an official of the executive branch of government, he should not be permitted to subpoena materials held by the president. Jaworski argued that neither the president nor anyone else was exempt from providing evidence needed for a criminal investigation. It was also pointed out that Alexander Haig had specifically promised Jaworski before he took the special prosecutor's job that he would have the right to sue to obtain presidential documents. Sirica decided in Jaworski's favor, ordering Nixon to surrender the sixty-four tapes.

Nixon appealed the ruling to the U.S. Court of Appeals. But Jaworski, contending that an immediate resolution of the dispute was urgent, asked the Supreme Court to bypass the appeals court and take jurisdiction over the case. The Supreme Court agreed and set arguments in the case for July 8.

In pleading his case before the Court, Jaworski emphasized the importance of demonstrating that the president was not above the law. St. Clair countered that Nixon did not claim to be above the law, but that the only way the law could be applied to the president was through impeachment.

Under questioning by Justice Thurgood Marshall, St. Clair declined to say flatly that Nixon would abide by the Court's decision in the case. When Marshall asked whether the president was "leaving it up to the Court to decide" the issue of the subpoenaed tapes, St. Clair replied, "Yes, in a sense." Asked to elaborate, he said: "In the sense that this Court has the obligation to determine the law. The President also has an obligation to carry out his constitutional duties." Pressed on the point later by news reporters, St. Clair said Nixon would obey an order to surrender the tapes if he decided it was in the public interest.

The point remained unresolved as the Supreme Court justices retired to ponder the issues. Meanwhile, the House Judiciary Committee continued its impeachment investigation. The committee had thirty-eight members—twenty-one Democrats and seventeen Republicans. Thus, if all the Democrats voted to recommend impeachment, there would be enough votes to send the matter to the full House for consideration.

Chairman Rodino, however, wanted to avoid having the committee vote strictly according to party affiliation. Such a division, he knew, would greatly diminish the likelihood of a House vote in favor of impeachment and a Senate vote for conviction. Accordingly, Rodino concentrated on swinging at least a handful of Republican committee votes in favor of impeachment.

The fact-finding portion of the committee's work proceeded for weeks behind closed doors. Each committee member was provided by the staff with three dozen loose-leaf notebooks filled with so-called statements of information concerning the case against Nixon. Day after day, Counsel Doar read excerpts from the books to the members and provided them with evidence backing the allegations. White House lawyer St. Clair was permitted to attend the meetings but was allowed to interrupt the proceedings only to make procedural points.

236

It was a dull, time-consuming process. Rodino felt it was necessary, however, to build a case that was sufficiently solid to attract bipartisan support for impeachment. In addition to considering the "statements of information" and documentary evidence, the committee called ten witnesses—mostly former White House and CREEP officials—to testify. St. Clair was permitted to cross-examine them. He vigorously tried to undermine the testimony of the chief witness, John Dean, but Dean stuck to his story of Nixon's participation in the Watergate cover-up.

After the testimony ended, Doar presented the committee with a summary of the evidence and a set of proposed articles of impeachment. He emphasized that the committee should concentrate not on whether Nixon had committed a single specific impeachable offense but rather on whether the president's pattern of conduct violated his oath to "take care that the laws be faithfully executed." The chief counsel to Republican committee members, Samuel A. Garrison III, conceded that considerable evidence had been gathered against Nixon. But he said the main issue to be decided was whether the president's impeachment would serve the public interest.

On July 24 the Supreme Court announced its decision in the case in which Special Prosecutor Jaworski was seeking sixty-four White House tapes. By an 8-to-0 vote, the Court ruled in favor of Jaworski. (The ninth justice, William Rehnquist, disqualified himself from participating in the case because he had been a high Justice Department official in the Nixon administration before his appointment to the court.)

Chief Justice Warren Burger, who read the decision on the Court's behalf, said there was some constitutional validity to Nixon's claim of executive privilege. But allowing Nixon to withhold evidence clearly needed in a criminal proceeding, Burger said, would seriously impair the operation of the courts. The Court ordered Nixon to surrender the tapes to Sirica, who would then review them and give those that were relevant to Jaworski.

For a time, Nixon considered defying the Court's order. He knew there was a great deal of material damaging to his cause on the tapes. Most serious of all were his discussions with H. R. Haldeman on June 23, 1972, six days after the Watergate arrests. That tape made clear that the president had directed the cover-up from the outset and had ordered the CIA to ask the FBI to curb its Watergate investigation. It invalidated Nixon's many denials of participation in the cover-up.

Nixon had not previously allowed any of his aides to hear that tape. But now, in an attempt to get an adviser's assessment on whether it was so damaging it should be withheld, he asked White House lawyer J. Fred Buzhardt to listen to the recording. After hearing the tape, Buzhardt reported to Alexander Haig and James St. Clair that it absolutely destroyed the president's claims of innocence. He said the conversations on the tape sharply contrasted with material the White House had provided to the House Judiciary Committee. Buzhardt concluded that Nixon's presidency would come to an end soon after the tape was made public—

the only question being whether he would resign or be impeached.

Haig and St. Clair, who had not been permitted by Nixon to hear the tape, apparently felt Buzhardt was overstating its importance but relayed his assessment to the president. Nixon himself said he thought Buzhardt was exaggerating the seriousness of the situation. He discussed with St. Clair, Haig, and Press Secretary Ronald Ziegler the alternatives open to him on responding to the Supreme Court decision. In the end, however, they decided he would have to surrender the tapes.

St. Clair went before the television news cameras and read a statement from the president that said he was disappointed with the Supreme Court decision but would comply with it in all respects. He called Nixon's decision to surrender the tapes a demonstration of the president's belief in the rule of law.

A short time after St. Clair completed his statement, the House Judiciary Committee began its televised debate on the proposed impeachment. Chairman Rodino opened the proceedings with an appeal to his colleagues to uphold the Constitution. "Our judgment is not concerned with an individual but with a system of constitutional government," he said.

Congressman Harold Donohue of Massachusetts, second only to Rodino in seniority among the Democrats on the committee, introduced a set of impeachment articles drafted by committee members and staff aides. It was understood that these articles were probably imperfect and would need amendment. But they served the purpose of giving the committee a starting point for the debate.

Several committee members took pains in their opening remarks to argue that the country could ill afford to see the impeachment question decided on the basis of partisan political considerations. Congressman Robert McClory of Illinois, a leading Republican, said he had heard some observers contend that a Republican could never vote to impeach a Republican president. He called that view demeaning. Democratic Congressman Jack Brooks of Texas said it was a time to put partisanship aside. "We as well as the President are on trial for how faithfully we fulfill our constitutional responsibility."

After the debate had continued for two days, Democratic Congressman Paul Sarbanes of Maryland introduced a substitute first article of impeachment intended to meet objections some committee members had raised to the original first article proposed by Donohue. Sarbanes's lengthy substitute article said that Nixon had "made it his policy" to conduct the Watergate activities and cover-up, then followed with a rundown of the events; but the activities and allegations were clothed in generalities such as "making or causing to be made false or misleading statements," "withholding relevant and material evidence," "approving, condoning, acquiescing," and "interfering or endeavoring to interfere." The article concluded, "Wherefore, Richard M. Nixon, by such conduct, warrants impeachment and trial and removal from office."

Several of Nixon's Republican defenders on the committee—especially Congressman Charles Wiggins

240

of California and Charles Sandman of New Jersey—bitterly assailed Sarbanes's substitute article. They argued that the president could not defend himself unless the allegations against him were more specific.

Wiggins said the heart of Sarbanes's article was a charge that "the President made it his policy" to obstruct justice and interfere with investigations. "Would you please explain to this member of the committee and to the other members when and in what respect and how did the President declare that policy?" he asked.

It was a difficult question to answer. Neither Sarbanes nor anyone else contended that Nixon had ever formally declared such a policy. The point remained troublesome not only to Wiggins but also to some supporters of Sarbanes's article.

Rodino asked committee counsel Doar whether the staff's study of prior impeachments indicated a need for "specificity" in impeachment articles. "Mr. Chairman, in my judgment it is not necessary to be totally specific, and I think this article of impeachment meets the test of specificity," Doar replied.

Rodino said he felt further discussion of the need for specifics amounted to "begging of a question" that had been settled. The committee, however, was not yet ready to vote on Sarbanes's article. It recessed overnight.

The next day—Saturday, July 27—Republican Congressman Thomas Railsback of Illinois introduced an amendment designed to solve the problem caused by the use of the word "policy" in Sarbanes's impeachment article. He proposed replacing "policy" with

241

"course of conduct or plan." The amendment may have seemed trivial to some observers, but it was considered important by several committee members. It was adopted by a voice vote.

After additional debate, the committee finally got down to its first crucial vote—whether to substitute Sarbanes's impeachment article for the original article introduced by Donohue. The vote was 27 to 11 in favor of the substitution. All the Democrats voted "aye," as did six Republicans—Railsback, Hamilton Fish, Jr., of New York, Lawrence Hogan of Maryland, M. Caldwell Butler of Virginia, William Cohen of Maine, and Harold Froehlich of Wisconsin.

Minutes later, by an identical vote, the committee took the historic step of adopting the Sarbanes substitute as its first article of impeachment against the president. The fact that six committee Republicans had been willing to vote for impeachment seemed a bad omen for Nixon's chances in the full House and Senate. After adopting the article, the committee recessed until the following Monday, when it would consider additional impeachment articles.

During the recess, several committee members drafted a new second article to replace the original submitted by Donohue. The substitute article accused Nixon of numerous violations of his constitutional duty to "take care that the laws be faithfully executed." When the committee resumed its debate on July 29, Democratic Congressman William Hungate of Missouri introduced the new article.

It accused Nixon of repeatedly engaging in "conduct violating the constitutional rights of citizens" and

242

"impairing the due and proper administration of justice." Specifically, the president was charged with misusing such agencies as the Internal Revenue Service, the FBI, the Secret Service, the CIA, and the Justice Department.

The committee voted to accept the Hungate substitute and adopt it as the second article of impeachment. This time, the tally was 28 to 10, with Republican Congressman McClory voting "aye" along with all those who had previously approved the first article. The following day, the committee adopted a third impeachment article introduced by McClory that accused Nixon of illegally defying committee subpoenas. Two other proposed articles were defeated. One accused Nixon of personal income-tax violations; the other charged him with improperly ordering the secret bombing of Cambodia during the Vietnam war. Except for the preparation of the report that was to be submitted to the full House along with the impeachment articles, the committee's work was finished.

Democratic and Republican leaders of the House agreed to begin the impeachment debate on August 19. They allocated eighty-seven hours for debate and hoped to bring the impeachment issue to a vote by early September. A handful of House members set to work on drafting the rules under which the debate would be conducted.

Meanwhile, new attention focused on the tapes Nixon had been ordered by the Supreme Court to surrender. Presidential attorney James St. Clair, in meetings with Judge Sirica and Special Prosecutor Jaworski, agreed to begin delivering the tapes to the court. Sirica was surprised to learn, in questioning St. Clair, that he had not personally listened to the tapes. He ordered St. Clair to do so.

Thus, a short time later, St. Clair finally heard the tape of Nixon's discussions with H. R. Haldeman on June 23, 1972. To his shock and dismay, St. Clair now realized that his fellow White House lawyer, J. Fred Buzhardt, had not been exaggerating in his previous assessment of the seriousness of the evidence on the tape. He concluded that Nixon's days in the presidency were numbered.

St. Clair provided White House chief of staff Alexander Haig with transcripts of the Nixon-Haldeman conversations. Haig, too, quickly reached the conclusion that Nixon could not long remain in office once the tape became public. He felt the president did not recognize the seriousness of the situation and decided to take matters partly into his own hands.

One of Haig's first steps was to go to Vice President Gerald R. Ford and alert him to the strong likelihood that he would soon be called upon to assume the presidency. (Nixon had appointed Ford to succeed Vice President Spiro T. Agnew, who had resigned after pleading no contest to tax-evasion charges stemming from a scandal dating back to his prior service as governor of Maryland.) Ford had staunchly defended Nixon throughout the Watergate affair, insisting that the president was totally innocent of involvement in the cover-up. Haig feared that if Ford continued to make an all-out defense of Nixon, he would suffer a severe loss of public confidence in the event he was elevated to the presidency.

At their meeting, Haig warned Ford about the hazards of making additional statements on Nixon's behalf. He described the conversations on the June 23 tape and labeled them as "catastrophic" to Nixon's chances of remaining in office. Haig said various White House staffers differed on the course the president should take. Some felt he should resign, but others thought he should fight to the end against removal. Haig asked if Ford had any advice on the matter. But Ford, after pondering for a while, said he thought it would be inappropriate for him to make any recommendation "that might cause a change in my status as Vice President." Similarly, he declined to make any suggestions on how to arrange a smooth transition if he replaced Nixon. Ford later said he had been "stunned" by the information Haig had given him—concerning both the evidence on the tape and the likelihood of his imminent elevation to the presidency.

The more Haig thought about the situation, the more he felt Nixon should resign. But he did not consider it wise to make such a suggestion directly. Instead, he tried working indirectly to bring about the resignation.

On August 2 Haig and St. Clair met with one of Nixon's most outspoken defenders on the House Judiciary Committee, Congressman Charles Wiggins. They showed him the transcripts of the most damaging portions of the June 23 tape. Wiggins read them several times, then said it was clear he and other Nixon loyalists had been "led down the garden path" by the president. Once the transcripts were made public, Wiggins said, the House impeachment debate would be-

245

come "almost academic." He foresaw a strong likelihood that the Senate would vote to convict Nixon and remove him from office. Finally, Wiggins said he thought it would be appropriate "to consider the resignation of the President." This message was eventually relayed to Nixon. Wiggins would later say he had never been told by Haig and St. Clair why they showed him the transcripts. "But I'm quite sure they wanted to get the reaction of one member of the committee," he said.

Having obtained Wiggins's reaction, Haig began passing word of the transcripts' contents to other diehard Nixon supporters. In a call to Senator Robert Griffin of Michigan, a member of the Senate Republican leadership, he described in detail the Nixon-Haldeman discussions.

Griffin decided to write a sternly worded letter to the president. The letter gave no indication that Griffin knew the contents of the transcripts but cautioned Nixon that his prospects for escaping conviction in a Senate vote were shaky at best. He said the Senate would subpoena numerous presidential tapes, including many denied to the House Judiciary Committee, for the trial. And if Nixon defied such a subpoena, Griffin said, "I shall regard that as an impeachable offense and shall vote accordingly." The strong tone of the letter—coming from a man Nixon had regarded as a staunch supporter—served as a fresh jolt to the president.

Next, Haig showed the June 23 transcripts to presidential speech writers Raymond Price and Patrick Buchanan. Price immediately concluded that "the

President ought to resign as quickly as possible" and asked Haig to relay that message to Nixon. Buchanan, although equally shocked by the transcripts, advised that Nixon make the new evidence public and then wait for the reaction before deciding on his next move.

Despite the recommendations from close political associates that he resign, Nixon was still unwilling to do so. He decided, instead, to release the transcripts of the conversations with Haldeman and make another plea for the public to rally behind him. At first, he intended to deliver the plea in a nationally televised address. But at the urging of his aides, he abandoned that idea and simply prepared a written statement to be issued with the transcripts.

On August 5 the transcripts and the statement were released at the White House. The statement said in part:

> I have today instructed my attorneys to make available to the House Judiciary Committee, and I am making public, the transcripts of three conversations with H. R. Haldeman on June 23, 1972. I have also turned over the tapes of these conversations to Judge Sirica. . . .
>
> It appears at this stage . . . that a House vote of impeachment is, as a practical matter, virtually a foregone conclusion, and that the issue will therefore go to trial in the Senate. . . . I recognize that this additional material I am now furnishing may further damage my case, especially because attention will be drawn separately to it rather than to the evidence in its entirety. . . .

247

I would urge that the evidence be looked at in its entirety and the events be looked at in perspective. Whatever mistakes I made in the handling of Watergate, the basic truth remains that when all the facts were brought to my attention I insisted on a full investigation and prosecution of those guilty. I am firmly convinced that the record, in its entirety, does not justify the extreme step of impeachment and removal of a President. I trust that as the constitutional process goes forward this perspective will prevail.

Any hopes Nixon harbored that the statement would soften the impact of the transcripts themselves were soon dashed. The release of the transcripts produced a jolting new wave of public defections from the Nixon camp. Even the remaining Republican members of the House Judiciary Committee who had voted against impeachment now joined the clamor for resignation.

Nonetheless, when Nixon met with his cabinet the day after he released the transcripts, he said he had thought about resigning but had decided to try to remain in office. "The Constitution makes no provision for resignation," he noted.

But the pressure for a resignation continued to build. Some of the Senate's most influential Republicans met and agreed there was no choice except for Nixon to resign. They saw no chance that he could survive a Senate vote to convict and remove him. Since a two-thirds vote was required in the Senate to oust the president, he needed the support of at least thirty-four senators to remain in office. Those present at the

248

meeting doubted he could pick up even half that many votes. It was decided that Senator Barry Goldwater of Arizona, the 1964 Republican presidential candidate, should seek a meeting with the president to outline the group's views.

Meanwhile, Nixon received another heavy blow when Republican National Chairman George Bush called for his resignation. In a letter he delivered to the White House, Bush told the president:

> My own view is that I would now ill serve a President, whose massive accomplishments I will always respect and whose family I love, if I did not give you my judgment. Until this morning resignation has been no answer at all, but given the impact of the latest development, and it will be a lasting one, I now firmly feel resignation is best for this country, best for this President.

The meeting Senator Goldwater had requested with the president was scheduled for the afternoon of August 7. At the suggestion of White House aides, Senate Republican Leader Hugh Scott of Pennsylvania and House Republican Leader John Rhodes of Arizona were also invited to attend. Just before the three men entered the Oval Office, Alexander Haig called them aside and urged them not to press Nixon directly to resign. Haig said the president had been reassessing his position and was "almost on the edge" of resignation. "If you suggest it, he may take umbrage and reverse," he warned.

249

When the meeting began, Nixon asked his three visitors to "be objective" in assessing the situation confronting him. In a clear reference to the possibility of resignation, he said: "I have a decision to make. What I need is your appraisal of the floor [of Congress]." He said he understood he could count on no more than 10 of the 435 members of the House to vote against impeachment. Congressman Rhodes felt the actual number might be about 50, but he did not say so because that figure was still far below the 218 votes needed. He contented himself with telling Nixon there might be more than 10 anti-impeachment votes, "but not much more."

As for the Senate, Goldwater told him: "I don't think you can count on more than fifteen votes." Scott estimated that "twelve or fifteen" senators would support Nixon to the bitter end. Goldwater hammered the point home by ticking off the names of one senator after another—long-time backers of the president—who would vote to convict him at a trial. Scott said the situation was "gloomy."

"It sounds damn gloomy," Nixon replied.

"Hopeless," Goldwater said.

Just before the meeting broke up, Nixon indicated that he considered resignation the only course left to him. "I just wanted to hear it from you," he said. Although his visitors had never specifically suggested resignation, the tone of the discussion left no doubt they felt that would be the proper decision.

Early that evening, Nixon told Haig he had definitely decided to resign. At dinner, he told his wife, two daughters, and sons-in-law of the decision. One daughter, Julie Nixon Eisenhower, argued strongly against quitting. But the president said he had no other choice and that the decision was final.

The next morning, Nixon invited Ford to the Oval Office and informed him he would become president the following day. "Jerry, you'll do a good job," Nixon said. Ford asked for suggestions on how to carry out the presidential duties under the circumstances in which he would be taking office. The two men talked for more than an hour, mostly about foreign policy.

Arrangements were made for Nixon to address the nation over television and radio at 9 o'clock that night. Although the advance announcement did not spell out the subject matter, there was wide speculation that he would declare his intention to resign. Haig began notifying the president's staff and advisers of the resignation decision.

At 7:30 P.M., Nixon met with the Democratic and Republican leaders of Congress to bid his farewell. Next, he received forty-six of his most loyal supporters from Capitol Hill. It was a melancholy scene as he thanked them for their help over the years. He said he would have liked to fight to the end against impeachment but had decided he had no choice except resignation. "I just hope that you don't feel that I let you down," he said, breaking into tears. Almost everyone else in the room cried along with him. Moments later, still sobbing, the president walked from the room.

But he regained his composure by the time he faced the television cameras about a half hour later. He was seated behind his desk in the Oval Office—seemingly in full control of his emotions—when his picture was beamed into households throughout the country and even beyond:

This is the thirty-seventh time I have spoken to you from this office in which so many decisions have been made that shape the history of this nation.

Each time I have done so to discuss with you some matters that I believe affected the national interest. And [in] all the decisions I have made in my public life I have always tried to do what was best for the nation.

Throughout the long and difficult period of Watergate, I have felt it was my duty to persevere; to make every possible effort to complete the term of office to which you elected me. In the past few days, however, it has become evident to me that I no longer have a strong enough political base in the Congress to justify continuing that effort.

As long as there was such a base, I felt strongly that it was necessary to see the constitutional process through to its conclusion; that to do otherwise would be unfaithful to the spirit of that deliberately difficult process, and a dangerously destabilizing precedent for the future. But, with the disappearance of that base, I now believe that the constitutional purpose has been served. And there is no longer a need for the process to be prolonged.

I would have preferred to carry through to the finish, whatever the personal agony it would have involved. . . . But the interests of the nation must always come before any personal considerations. From the discussions I have had with congressional and other leaders, I have concluded that because of the Watergate matter I might not have the support of the Congress that I would consider necessary to back the very difficult decisions and carry out the duties of this office in the way the interests of the nation will require.

I have never been a quitter. To leave office before my term is completed is opposed to every instinct in my body. But as President I must put the interests of America first.

America needs a full-time President and a full-time Congress, particularly at this time with problems we face at home and abroad. To continue to fight through the months ahead for my personal vindication would almost totally absorb the time and attention of both the President and the Congress in a period when our entire focus should be on the great issues of peace abroad and prosperity without inflation at home.

Therefore, I shall resign the presidency effective at noon tomorrow.

Vice President Ford will be sworn in as President at that hour in this office.

As I recall the high hopes for America with which we began this second term, I feel a great sadness that I will not be here in this office working on your behalf to achieve those hopes in the next two and a half years. But in turning over direction of the government to Vice President

Ford I know, as I told the nation when I nominated him for that office ten months ago, that the leadership of America will be in good hands. . . .

By taking this action, I hope that I will have hastened the start of that process of healing which is so desperately needed in America. I regret deeply any injuries that have been done in the course of the events that led to this decision. I would say only that if some of my judgments were wrong—and some were wrong—they were made in what I believed at the time to be the best interests of the nation.

To those who have stood with me during these past difficult months, to my family, my friends, the many others who've joined in supporting my cause because they believed it was right, I will be eternally grateful for your support. And to those who have not felt able to give me your support, let me say I leave with no bitterness toward those who have opposed me, because all of us in the final analysis have been concerned with the good of the country, however our judgments might differ.

So let us all now join together in affirming that common commitment and in helping our new President succeed for the benefit of all Americans. I shall leave this office with regret at not completing my term but with gratitude for the privilege of serving as your President for the past five and a half years. . . .

To have served in this office is to have felt a very personal sense of kinship with each and every American. In leaving it, I do so with this prayer: May God's grace be with you all in the days ahead.

After the speech, Nixon and his wife took a final tour of the White House. He then stayed up late into the night, telephoning friends to thank them for their support and seek reassurance that he had made the right move in resigning.

The next morning, he delivered an emotional farewell talk to the White House staff. Afterward, he and his wife boarded the presidential aircraft for a flight to their home in San Clemente, California. At 11:30 A.M., while the Nixons were in the air, a letter was delivered according to protocol to Secretary of State Henry Kissinger. "Dear Mr. Secretary," it said. "I hereby resign the office of President of the United States. Sincerely, Richard Nixon." Precisely at noon, as the Nixon plane passed over Jefferson City, Missouri, Gerald R. Ford was sworn in as president by Chief Justice Warren Burger in the Oval Office.

In his inaugural address, Ford took note of the extraordinary circumstances that had brought him to the presidency:

My fellow Americans, our long national nightmare is over. Our Constitution works. Our great republic is a government of laws and not of men. Here, the people rule. . . . As we bind up the internal wounds of Watergate, more painful and more poisonous than those of foreign wars, let us restore the Golden Rule to our political

255

process. And let brotherly love purge our hearts of suspicion and hate.

Actually, the "nightmare" was not quite over. Some loose ends remaining from the Watergate affair were still to be tied. Criminal proceedings against several defendants were still pending. And Ford would stir new controversy by granting Nixon a pardon for any crimes the former president might have committed while in office. But there was no question that Nixon's resignation and Ford's assumption of the presidency went a long way toward "putting Watergate behind us."

The major questions remaining were what the nation had learned from Watergate and what it would do to prevent similar "nightmares" in the future.

PART FOUR
MOVES
FOR REFORM

14 POST-WATERGATE MORALITY

As might have been expected, the Watergate affair prompted a flood of demands for reform of the American political system. Countless public officials, candidates, political party functionaries, journalists, public-interest organizations and private individuals weighed in with proposals aimed at guaranteeing that the nation would never again be plagued by such a scandal.

Most of the suggested reforms were serious, a few frivolous. Many were worthy in purpose but almost impossible to enact or enforce. By far the most extensive reforms—and those that received the widest public attention—were proposed by the Senate Watergate Committee. In concluding its seventeen-month investigation, the committee issued a 2,217-page report chock full of suggestions for sweeping new campaign laws and regulations and calling for the enforcement of the criminal laws "against all offenders—even those of high estate."

One of the committee's major recommendations called for creation of a permanent special prosecutor's office. The committee proposed that the new position, to be called the public attorney's office, be given jurisdiction over prosecuting all "criminal cases in which there is a real or apparent conflict of interest" within the executive branch. "The public attorney would also have jurisdiction to inquire into . . . the status and progress of complaints and criminal charges pending in or involving the conduct of federal departments and regulatory agencies."

To ensure that the proposed office would be independent of the executive branch, the committee recommended that the public attorney be chosen by the judiciary. Under the committee's plan, the chief justice of the Supreme Court would choose three retired judges of the U.S. Court of Appeals who would, in turn, select the public attorney. The public attorney would serve for a fixed term, which the committee suggested should last five years.

The committee found that one of the major elements making the Watergate affair possible was the loose government regulation of the financing of election campaigns. Vast amounts of money had been secretly shuffled about among participants in the political-spying operation and the cover-up. Moreover, investigation revealed that hundreds of thousands of dollars had been contributed illegally to President Nixon's re-election campaign and the coffers of other candidates, Democrats and Republicans alike. Many such illegal contributions had come from corporations, which were forbidden by law to donate to federal election campaigns, and had been laundered to make the money difficult to trace.

To correct such abuses, the committee recommended the establishment of an independent, nonpartisan Federal Election Commission that would oversee campaign financing and expenditures. Creation of such a commission would probably be "the most significant reform that could emerge from the Watergate scandal," the committee report said.

The committee also recommended a series of companion measures aimed at tightening regulation of campaign financing. One such measure required that each candidate for president or vice president designate one political committee as his central campaign committee. The purpose was to bar candidates from using numerous political committees to raise and spend funds —a practice that made it extremely difficult for investigators to trace the money.

Another potential abuse pointed up in the committee report concerned the Nixon campaign's use of incumbent and former administration officials to solicit financial contributions from private citizens, many of them business executives over whom the officials exercised direct government authority. Under such circumstances, some executives naturally feared that they or their companies might suffer from government reprisals if they did not contribute. Conversely, others felt they might guarantee favored treatment from the government if they made contributions. To prevent

261

even the appearance of coercion, the committee recommended that no official whose appointment required Senate approval or who was on the payroll of the executive office of the president be permitted to participate in soliciting or receiving campaign contributions while employed by the government or for a year afterward.

In an effort to curb future political spying and dirty tricks, the committee urged passage of a broad range of new federal legislation. The report said, in part:

The committee recommends that Congress enact criminal legislation to prohibit anyone from obtaining employment, voluntary or paid, in a campaign of an individual seeking nomination or election to any federal office by false pretenses, misrepresentations or other fraudulent means for the purpose of interfering with, spying on or obstructing any campaign activities of such candidate.

Furthermore, such legislation should make it unlawful for anyone to direct, instruct or pay anyone to join any such campaign by such means or for such purposes as are outlined above. New legislation is needed to prevent the infiltration of presidential and federal campaigns. . . .

The committee recommends that Congress enact legislation to make it unlawful to request or knowingly to disburse or make available campaign funds for the purpose of promoting or financing violations of federal election laws. . . .

The committee recommends that Congress enact

new legislation which prohibits the theft, unauthorized copying or the taking by false pretenses of campaign materials, documents or papers not available for public dissemination belonging to or in the custody of a candidate for federal office or his aides. . . .

Other committee recommendations included making certain crimes ordinarily prosecuted by state authorities, such as burglary and larceny, federal offenses as well if committed with the intent of affecting an election; prohibiting all Justice Department employees, including the attorney general, from taking part in political activities (many government employees were already barred from such activities by a law called the Hatch Act); forbidding the president or his aides to establish special White House investigative operations, such as those carried out by the Plumbers unit, without authority from Congress; giving Congress greater power to supervise federal intelligence and law-enforcement agencies and their relationships with the White House; tightening federal laws on wiretapping and electronic bugging; and making it a felony for government officials to award federal contracts or grants in such a manner as to try to influence an election.

If all or even most of the reforms proposed by the Senate committee were put into effect, they might go a long way toward elevating American political practices and ensuring that the nation will never again be plagued by a scandal such as Watergate. Unfortunately, however, that has not happened. At this writing, more than three years after the Senate Watergate Committee

263

issued its report, most of its recommendations remain in the realm of mere proposals. Few have been enacted into law.

Officials of President Gerald Ford's administration opposed many of the proposals on the grounds that they were unnecessary or would duplicate steps being taken by the executive branch to clean its own house. Some members of Congress refused to back various recommendations, perhaps fearing that the proposed reforms might restrict their own political activities. Moreover, after the resignation of President Nixon, some of the fervor for reform faded. Many Americans, both public officials and private citizens, were weary of hearing about Watergate and its aftermath; they wanted to move on to other matters. All these factors contributed to preventing speedy adoption of many of the committee's suggestions.

One major committee proposal that did reach fruition involved the establishment of a Federal Election Commission. Legislation passed by Congress in 1974 created a six-member commission empowered to administer, interpret, and enforce federal campaign finance laws. The legislation provided for the president, the speaker of the House, and the president pro tem of the Senate each to appoint two members from opposing political parties. All the nominations required confirmation by majority votes of both houses of Congress. The commission members, whose terms were set at six years, were empowered to elect a chairman and vice-chairman from different political parties.

Those initially appointed to the commission were Thomas B. Curtis, a former Republican congressman from Missouri; Neil O. Staebler, a former Democratic congressman from Michigan; Joan D. Aikens, an advertising executive and former president of the Pennsylvania Council of Republican Women; Thomas E. Harris, a Virginia Democrat and former associate general counsel of the AFL–CIO; Vernon W. Thomson, a Republican who had served as a congressman and as governor of Wisconsin; and Robert O. Tiernan, a former Democratic congressman from Rhode Island. The commission elected Curtis as chairman and Staebler as vice-chairman.

Under the legislation, the commission was responsible for overseeing a complex new set of regulations governing campaign contributions and expenditures. Among other things, the law provided for the federal government—using tax funds—to assume a major part of the cost of financing presidential campaigns. The main purpose of the plan for federal subsidization of the campaigns was to eliminate the heavy reliance by presidential candidates on funds from so-called fat-cat contributors. Some of these wealthy contributors undoubtedly expected favors from government officials who reached office with the help of their donations. Even though such favoritism often could not be proved, the public was frequently left with the impression that relatively small groups of privileged individuals were exerting undue influence over the nation's political and governmental decisions.

The new legislation enabled every American taxpayer, by checking a box on his income tax return, to designate a dollar of his tax payment annually for use in financing presidential campaigns. A fund established

265

with this money was placed under the supervision of the Federal Election Commission.

To qualify for federal funds while running in presidential primaries, a candidate was required to raise $5,000 through private contributions in each of twenty states. The government would then provide the candidate with matching funds based on the contributions he received from private sources during the primary period. Each contribution up to $250 from a private individual would be matched by the government. Contributors would be permitted to donate up to $1,000 each to any candidate during the primary period, but only the first $250 would be eligible for matching funds. Each presidential candidate would be limited to spending a total of $10 million for all his primary campaigns—plus up to $2 million for fund raising.

In general elections, the new law provided for virtually full federal financing of the campaigns of major-party nominees—that is, the Democratic and Republican presidential candidates. A basic spending limit of $20 million was set for each candidate during the general-election campaign. Candidates of major parties automatically would qualify to receive $20 million in federal funds. Minor-party presidential candidates would be eligible for lesser amounts, to be determined by the number of votes the party received in past elections. Acceptance of the federal funds was made optional, but any candidate taking the full $20 million would be barred from collecting private contributions for the general election. Any candidate who declined the government funds or did not receive the full $20 million in federal aid would be allowed to spend up to $4 million on fund raising.

In addition to the money spent directly by a candidate's campaign organization, each national political party—major or minor—would be allowed to spend up to $2.9 million on behalf of its presidential nominee. The new law also provided for use of federal funds to defray the cost of conducting national political conventions. Major parties would automatically qualify for $2 million each toward their convention expenses. Minor parties would be eligible for lesser amounts based on the number of votes received in the previous presidential election.

Although the new legislation did not provide for federal financing of Senate and House campaigns, it did place limits on contributions and spending in those races. Again, one of the major purposes of the limits was to reduce the influence of wealthy contributors on the political process. An individual was permitted to contribute no more than $1,000 to the primary campaign of a Senate or House candidate and no more than another $1,000 toward the candidate's general-election campaign. Moreover, no individual was allowed to contribute more than $25,000 during any campaign year to all federal campaigns combined— that is, presidential, senatorial, and congressional races.

In senatorial primary campaigns, each candidate was permitted to spend $100,000 or eight cents for every citizen of voting age in his state, whichever was higher. An additional amount, up to 20 percent of the basic limit, was allowed for fund raising. In senatorial general-election campaigns, a candidate was authorized to spend $150,000 or twelve cents for each voting-age citizen in the state, whichever was higher. Again, he was allowed to spend up to 20 percent of the basic limit for fund raising. In both House primary and general-election campaigns, the spending limits were identical —$70,000, plus $14,000 for fund raising.

Another provision of the new law sought to meet complaints that some wealthy candidates had virtually "bought" their way into office by investing enormous amounts of their own money in their campaigns. The law placed limits on how much candidates could contribute to their own campaigns—$50,000 for the presidency, $35,000 for the Senate, and $25,000 for the House.

The law required candidates, campaign organizations, political parties, and fund-raising committees to file detailed reports on contributions and expenditures regularly with the Federal Election Commission. Such reports were to be made available to the public and press. Individuals committing flagrant violations of the election finance law were subject to prison terms of up to five years and fines of up to $50,000. In addition, any candidate for federal office who failed to file the necessary reports could be barred from running again for a federal position during the term of the office that he was seeking, plus one year.

The Federal Election Commission launched its operations on April 14, 1975. It soon began issuing regulations on how the new legislation was to be administered. Within a short time, some of the rulings aroused strong opposition from various members of Congress.

These senators and representatives, many of whom

268

had originally voted to create the commission, now suddenly felt threatened by it. Some of them, at least, apparently feared the commission's rulings might pose threats to their own political careers. Speeches assailing the commission's methods of carrying out its duties were heard with increasing frequency from the floors of the House and Senate. Before long, the speeches were followed by legislative action aimed at undercutting the commission's authority.

Under the new legislation, any regulation drafted by the commission to implement the law was to take effect automatically if it was not disapproved by the House or Senate within thirty days. In quick succession, Congress voted down two regulations put forward by the commission. First, the Senate disapproved a regulation that would have enabled the commission to regulate so-called congressional "slush-funds"—made up of money given by private contributors to some senators and representatives to pay for miscellaneous expenses, such as the costs of travel and office supplies, over and above those provided by the government. Next, the House killed a regulation concerning the procedure the commission wanted members of Congress to follow in filing campaign finance reports.

These two setbacks were followed by other potential problems for the commission. Democratic Congressman Wayne Hays of Ohio, chairman of the House Administration Committee, introduced a legislative amendment intended to give Congress further control over the commission. Instead of permitting a regulation to become effective automatically unless disapproved within thirty days by the House or Senate, Hays's measure provided

269

that a regulation would automatically be killed unless both houses voted to approve it within thirty days. Such a requirement, if enacted, would have made it infinitely more difficult to put commission regulations into effect. With congressional calendars crowded by other business, the process of getting commission regulations voted upon by the House and Senate—much less approved—would have been a hit-and-miss proposition.

Commission Chairman Thomas Curtis protested that Hays's proposal, if approved, would turn the commission into "a toady of Congress." He called on leaders and members of Congress to reject the measure.

Heeding Curtis's warning, Congress refrained—at least temporarily—from adopting the Hays amendment. But the dispute underscored the hazards confronting the commission as it tried to carry out its assigned duties.

These hazards were further emphasized by still another serious challenge to the commission's authority. It came in a lawsuit seeking to have major portions of the law establishing the commission declared unconstitutional. The suit was filed by a group calling itself an admittedly "odd coalition" of persons from opposite ends of the political spectrum. Among those joining in the suit were then-Senator James Buckley of New York, who had been elected on the Republican and Conservative party tickets; former Senator Eugene McCarthy of Minnesota, a liberal Democrat who had run unsuccessfully for president in 1968 and 1972 and planned to run as an independent presidential candidate in the 1976 campaign; Stewart Mott, a wealthy backer of liberal political and social causes; and the American Civil Liberties Union.

The suit charged that the very structure of the Federal Election Commission was unconstitutional. Since the commission was part of the executive branch, it said, the fact that four of the six commission members had been appointed by congressional leaders violated the separation-of-powers provision of the Constitution. The suit also claimed that the new campaign finance law discriminated against minor-party and independent candidates; that it gave unfair advantages to incumbents; that the ceilings on campaign contributions and expenditures represented unconstitutional infringements of free speech, since they curbed candidates' ability to pay for advertising and limited contributors' efforts to back politicians whose views they supported; and that the requirement that contributors of even minor amounts of money be identified in campaign finance reports invaded individuals' personal privacy. On these and other grounds, the suit asked the federal courts to overturn many of the new law's most important provisions.

After hearing evidence, lower courts upheld the constitutionality of the law—but the case was appealed to the Supreme Court. In November 1975, when the Supreme Court heard arguments in the case, most of the justices expressed concern that some provisions of the law might infringe on constitutional rights. They seemed particularly troubled by the contention that the limits on contributions and expenditures abridged free speech.

After hearing the arguments, the Supreme Court did not issue a decision until January 30, 1976. By that time, the presidential primary campaigns were under

271

way and the Federal Election Commission had begun distributing matching funds to candidates.

The Court ruled that important sections of the campaign finance law were indeed unconstitutional. To begin with, the justices agreed with the contention that the manner in which the commission was formed—with the president appointing two members and congressional leaders naming four others—violated the Constitution. In order for the commission's structure to comply with the Constitution's separation-of-powers provision, the Court held, Congress would have to pass new legislation authorizing the president to appoint all six members.

Upholding the argument that sections of the campaign finance law abridged free speech, the justices struck down some—but not all—of the limits on campaign spending and contributions. They ruled that a presidential candidate could spend as much money as he wanted on his campaign as long as he did not apply for federal matching funds. But if he did accept matching funds, he would have to abide by the financial limitations of the law. Since the law provided for no matching funds in Senate and House races, the Court ruled that the limitations on candidates for those offices were improper. Thus Senate and House candidates would be permitted to spend as much as they could legally collect.

The justices upheld the section of the law providing that an individual could *directly* contribute no more than $1,000 to any one federal candidate and no more than $25,000 to all federal candidates combined during a campaign year. But they ruled that there should be no limits on indirect, unauthorized spending by private citizens on behalf of candidates. As long as there was no prearrangement or coordination between a citizen and the candidate's organization, the Court said, the individual could spend to his heart's content. For example, he could buy numerous newspaper advertisements and television or radio commercials promoting the candidate's campaign, provided the candidate's organization played no role in the process.

The Court also struck down, in general, the limits in the law placed on the amounts of money candidates could contribute to their own campaigns. Except for presidential aspirants accepting matching funds—who would continue to be prohibited from investing more than $50,000 in their own campaigns—the justices ruled that candidates could spend as much of their own money as they chose.

Under the decision, Congress was given thirty days to pass new legislation reorganizing the Federal Election Commission along the lines set down by the Court. During those thirty days, the commission could continue operating generally as it had in the past and could continue distributing matching funds. But if Congress did not meet the deadline, the commission would automatically lose at least temporarily its enforcement powers and authority to distribute matching funds. It would retain only the power to collect and disseminate campaign finance information until Congress passed the legislation necessary to reorganize the commission and restore its previous authority.

The Supreme Court decision touched off broad confusion and controversy. Presidential candidates who had been depending on an uninterrupted flow of match-

273

ing funds with which to help run their campaigns had no way of knowing how long they would continue to receive the federal subsidies. Nobody could be sure precisely what authority the Federal Election Commission would have during the 1976 election campaigns and those that followed. There was dismay in some quarters over the manner in which the Court had relaxed the limitations on campaign contributions and expenditures. "The Fat Cat Society is back in business," said Election Commission Vice-Chairman Neil Staebler.

Some members of Congress—notably those who had been most critical of the commission in the past—showed no great zeal to pass the necessary reorganization legislation. Congressman Wayne Hays, for example, said his initial reaction to the court decision was to do nothing "and let the commission expire and give it a nice, quiet burial." Other members of the House and Senate, however, introduced bills aimed at rescuing the commission.

The trouble was that the various bills introduced contained widely conflicting provisions, and even those senators and congressmen who favored corrective legislation encountered difficulty in compromising these differences. Six senators, for example, introduced a measure that provided for reorganization of the commission but also contained a section seeking to establish federal subsidies for Senate elections. Meanwhile, Republican Congressman Bill Franzel of Minnesota introduced a bill omitting any provision for subsidies in Senate or House races.

While debate raged in Congress, the thirty-day deadline set by the Supreme Court passed. The Court

274

granted two extensions of the deadline—the second one lasting until March 22—but when Congress had not acted by that date the Election Commission was forced to halt the payment of matching funds. The cutoff of funds imposed a hardship on several presidential contenders, whose campaign treasuries desperately needed the federal subsidies. All major presidential hopefuls continued filing claims for matching funds with the commission, hoping the money would be paid as soon as possible after Congress passed the necessary legislation.

It took Congress until May 4 to agree on a compromise and push the new law through both houses. The legislation, which gave the president authority to appoint all six members of the Election Commission, omitted federal subsidies for House or Senate candidates. It contained new provisions requiring that matching funds be cut off to any presidential contender who failed to receive at least 10 percent of the votes in two consecutive primaries in which he actively competed; that the Election Commission simplify some of the rules governing the filing of candidates' financial reports; and that labor unions file reports with the commission on money spent to communicate with their members on behalf of favored candidates.

President Ford signed the new legislation on May 11. But the Election Commission could not resume full-scale operations until the president named its members, the Senate confirmed the appointments, and the commissioners took their oaths of office. Ford had announced he was prepared to reappoint the original six commission members. Chairman Thomas Curtis, how-

275

ever, informed the president he no longer wanted to
serve on the commission. Thus there was a further delay while Ford decided on a replacement for Curtis. He
eventually chose William L. Springer, a former Republican congressman from Illinois. After Springer and the
five remaining original commission members were officially named by the president, the Senate quickly confirmed the appointments. The commissioners were
finally sworn in on May 21 and elected Vernon Thomson as the new chairman.

The commission immediately began distributing the
long-delayed matching funds to presidential contenders.
Nine candidates collected a total of more than $3.2
million in back payments. The chief beneficiary was
President Ford himself, who received $1.3 million to-
ward his campaign for a four-year presidential term of
his own. His rival for the Republican presidential nomination, former California Governor Ronald Reagan,
got more than $500,000. Among the Democratic presi-
dential contenders, former Georgia Governor Jimmy
Carter received the biggest subsidy, $437,000, and
Arizona Congressman Morris Udall was second with
$312,000.

Despite all the problems that cropped up in putting
the new election finance legislation into effect, there
was general agreement that the law worked reasonably
well in its first test during the 1976 election campaigns.
Candidates' reliance on large donations from wealthy
contributors was substantially reduced, thus curbing
the presumed obligations of office seekers to persons
with vested interests. There was a more even distribution of money to rival candidates than in previous elec-

tions. And the extensive record keeping, overseen by the Federal Election Commission, made it possible for the public to know much more than ever before about precisely how campaign money was raised and spent.

In the jockeying for the presidency, former Governor Carter—although little-known previously on the national scene—ran exceptionally well in the primaries and won the Democratic nomination. President Ford, despite strong opposition from former Governor Reagan, captured the Republican nomination. Although Carter started the general-election campaign with a wide lead in the public opinion polls, Ford narrowed the gap as election day approached. Ford was hurt in the campaign by the sluggish state of the nation's economy—particularly the high rates of unemployment and inflation. In addition, although he had not been personally involved in the Watergate affair, his membership in the scandal-scarred Nixon administration undoubtedly worked to his disadvantage—as may have his pardon of the former president. Carter ultimately won the election by a slender margin.

All told, the Federal Election Commission distributed more than $72 million to help finance the primary and general-election campaigns for president. Political experts said the new election finance law had exerted a profound influence on the presidential race. The matching funds provided during the primaries had helped Carter rise from relative obscurity to national prominence, allowing him to overcome an initially narrow base of geographical and financial support. Similarly, matching funds had aided Reagan in mounting an unusually strong primary challenge against an incumbent president—thus sharply dividing the Republican Party and further damaging Ford's chances in the general election. The ceiling on campaign spending apparently worked to the advantage of the Democratic nominee. In previous presidential elections, Republican candidates—largely because of their backing from wealthy business executives—had usually been able to spend considerably more money than their Democratic opponents. There was little doubt that Ford's campaign could have raised more money than Carter's if the spending ceiling and federal subsidies had not been in effect.

As a result of the ceiling, spending by both major candidates was held well below the amounts spent in prior presidential campaigns. The $22 million each spent on the general election by Carter and Ford (including money allocated by the Democratic and Republican national committees) did not even approach the $60 million campaign by President Nixon in 1972 or the $30 million campaign of his Democratic opponent, Senator George McGovern. The most noticeable effect of the lower amounts of available money came in a lack of campaign paraphernalia—such as buttons, bumper stickers, billboards, and leaflets. The Ford and Carter forces decided to do without large supplies of such materials and concentrate their spending instead on purchase of television and radio commercials.

After the election, still more proposals were made for revising the campaign finance law. Some members of Congress—contending that the amounts of money available to the 1976 presidential candidates had been inadequate—suggested increasing the federal subsidies to the two major-party nominees by a minimum of $5

278

million and perhaps as much as $8 million to $13 million. Others proposed increasing the amount an individual could contribute to a presidential candidate's primary campaign from $1,000 to as much as $5,000. There was some sentiment in favor of increasing the limit on individual contributions to House and Senate candidates in similar fashion, but a number of congressmen argued that was unnecessary because of the lower cost of congressional races.

Renewed pressure also arose for providing federal subsidies to House and Senate candidates. The proposal with the greatest apparent support called for a system of matching funds for use only in general elections. To qualify for the funds, a candidate would have to raise $5,000 in gifts of $100 or less. After that, under the proposal, the government would match the first $100 of every additional private contribution the candidate received. The subsidies would be accompanied by new spending limits in House and Senate races.

All the proposed revisions in the law are still under consideration at this writing, and it is not yet clear which—if any—of them will be enacted. But it seems certain that the general guidelines under which the Federal Election Commission operated during 1976 will become fixtures in future elections.

In addition to the federal campaign finance legislation, thirty states have passed their own laws limiting contributions and expenditures in campaigns for state offices. Three of the states—New Jersey, Maryland, and Minnesota—provide subsidies to candidates for such offices.

As a probable result of the notoriety given the Water-

279

gate scandal, the 1976 elections saw a sharp drop in the number of reported incidents of dirty politics. The Fair Campaign Practices Committee said it received fewer complaints in 1976 than in any year since it began monitoring campaigns in 1954. The forty-two complaints received were precisely half the number filed in the Watergate year of 1972. Of course, to those who claimed they were the victims of dirty campaigning, every complaint was one too many.

In addition, federal authorities charged that fraud and other illegal practices occurred during several 1976 elections. In Louisiana, for example, nineteen election commissioners were indicted on charges of falsifying hundreds of votes in order to ensure the victory of Richard A. Tonry, a former state legislator, in a Democratic congressional primary. Tonry himself was later indicted on charges of soliciting and concealing illegal campaign contributions. By that time, he had won the general election and taken his seat in Congress. He resigned after serving only four months in Congress, entered a guilty plea, and was sent to prison for a year.

In another case, the U.S. Justice Department filed a suit accusing the county government in Uvalde County, Texas, of redrawing election-district lines in such a way as to discriminate against Mexican-American voters in elections for county commissioners' jobs. The suit contended that the redistricting violated the Voting Rights Act of 1965. A similar suit accused officials in Sheffield, Alabama, of adopting procedures that discriminated against black voters in city elections.

Although the number of complaints about dirty politics decreased in 1976, some experts predicted that the decline would be merely temporary. As the Watergate scandal became an ever more distant memory, these experts feared, many politicians would resort anew to the sort of dirty tricks that marred past campaigns.

To combat that expected trend, public officials would do well to adopt many of the thus far neglected reforms proposed by the Senate Watergate Committee and others:

There is still a need for an independent, permanent special prosecutor's office in the federal government.

There is still a need for federal legislation barring political organizations from planting spies in their opponents' campaign staffs.

There is still a need for legislation making it a crime to steal confidential campaign documents.

There is still a need for a law making it illegal for a person to claim falsely that he represents a candidate with the intention of hurting the candidate's campaign.

There is still a need for legislation barring campaign officials from making campaign funds available to finance violations of election laws.

There is still a need to prohibit Justice Department employees from participating in political activities.

There is still a need to tighten laws against wiretapping and electronic bugging. And there is still a need for enactment of numerous other reforms.

Of course, reform measures alone cannot rid the nation of the evils of dirty politics. As the Senate Watergate Committee's final report put it:

Improper and unethical [campaign] activities . . . will not be eliminated merely by new legislation.

281

Although law seeks both to shape and reflect the moral and ethical values of individuals, new laws cannot fully substitute for such individual values. Therefore, the political process and government itself must attract individuals of the highest moral and ethical standards if improper activities . . . are to be eliminated completely in the future.

It is up to the American people to demonstrate that they demand the "highest moral and ethical standards" from their political leaders. It is up to them to become sufficiently involved in the political process to be able to choose leaders who meet such standards. And since a political system usually mirrors the values of society, it is up to the people to show that they adhere to such standards in their own lives. Only then can the nation hope to eliminate of the scourge of dirty politics.

ACKNOWLEDGMENTS ══

This book could not have been written without the valuable information and insights gathered from interviews and conversations with officials of the White House and the U.S. Secret Service, with members of the Senate Watergate Committee and the House Judiciary Committee, as well as other political figures, and with fellow journalists and authors. To all of them my heartfelt thanks.

At Delacorte Press, my thanks to Ross Claiborne, Ron Buehl, Alice Bregman, and Amy Ehrlich. Thanks also to Marilyn Meeker and Dorothy Markinko.

My wife, Jeanne, and daughters, Pamela and Patricia, saw me through the researching and writing of the book with eternal patience and good humor.

BIBLIOGRAPHY

Alexander, Herbert E. *Money in Politics.* Washington, D.C.: Public Affairs Press, 1972.

Breslin, Jimmy. *How the Good Guys Finally Won.* New York: Viking Press, 1975.

Chester, Lewis; McCrystal, Cal; and Aris, Stephen. *Watergate.* New York: Ballantine Books, 1973.

Colson, Charles W. *Born Again.* Old Tappan, N.J.: Chosen Books, 1976.

Cook, Fred J. *American Political Bosses and Machines.* New York: Franklin Watts, 1973.

Dean, John W. *Blind Ambition: The White House Years.* New York: Simon and Schuster, 1976.

Felknor, Bruce L. *Dirty Politics.* New York: W. W. Norton, 1966.

House Judiciary Committee. *Hearings and Final Report on the Impeachment of Richard M. Nixon.* Washington, D.C.: Government Printing Office, 1974.

Hunt, Howard E. *Undercover: Memoirs of an American Secret Agent.* New York: Berkley Publishing Corp., 1974.

————. *Give Us This Day*. New York: Popular Library, 1974.

Jaworski, Leon. *The Right and the Power: The Prosecution of Watergate*. New York: Reader's Digest Press, 1976.

Lasky, Victor. *It Didn't Start with Watergate*. New York: Dial Press, 1977.

Lavine, Harold, ed. *Smoke-Filled Rooms*. Englewood Cliffs, N.J.: Prentice-Hall, 1970.

Lukas, J. Anthony. *Nightmare: The Underside of the Nixon Years*. New York: Viking Press, 1976.

Lurie, Leonard. *The Impeachment of Richard Nixon*. New York: Berkley Publishing Corp., 1973.

————. *The Running of Richard Nixon*. New York: Coward, McCann & Geoghegan, 1972.

MacNeil, Robert. *The People Machine*. New York: Harper & Row, 1968.

Magruder, Jeb S. *An American Life: One Man's Road to Watergate*. New York: Atheneum, 1974.

Mankiewicz, Frank. *Perfectly Clear: Nixon from Whittier to Watergate*. New York: Quadrangle, 1973.

————. *U.S. vs. Richard M. Nixon: The Final Crisis*. New York: Quadrangle, 1975.

Martin, Ralph G. *The Bosses*. New York: Putnam, 1964.

McCarthy, Mary. *The Mask of State: Watergate Portraits*. New York: Harcourt Brace Jovanovich, 1974.

McCarthy, Max. *Elections for Sale*. New York: Houghton Mifflin, 1972.

McCord, James W., Jr. *A Piece of Tape*. Rockville, Md.: Washington Media Services, 1974.

New York Times Staff. *The End of a Presidency*. New York: Bantam Books, 1974.

O'Brien, Lawrence F. *No Final Victories: A Life in Politics from John F. Kennedy to Watergate*. New York: Doubleday, 1974.

Osborne, John. *The Last Nixon Watch*. Washington, D.C.: New Republic Book Co., 1975.

Phillips, Kevin. *The Emerging Republican Majority*. New Rochelle, N.Y.: Arlington House, 1969.

Rather, Dan, and Gates, Gary P. *The Palace Guard*. New York: Harper & Row, 1974.

Safire, William. *Before the Fall: An Inside View of the Pre-Watergate White House*. New York: Doubleday, 1975.

Schrag, Peter. *Test of Loyalty*. New York: Simon and Schuster, 1974.

Senate Select Committee on Presidential Campaign Activities. *Hearings* and *Final Report*. Washington, D.C.: Government Printing Office, 1973.

Sussman, Barry. *The Great Cover-Up: Nixon and the Scandal of Watergate*. New York: T. Y. Crowell, 1974.

Szulc, Tad. *Compulsive Spy: The Strange Career of E. Howard Hunt*. New York: Viking Press, 1974.

Thayer, George. *Who Shakes the Money Tree?* New York: Simon and Schuster, 1973.

Thompson, Fred D. *At That Point in Time: The Inside Story of the Senate Watergate Committee*. New York: Quadrangle, 1975.

Washington Post Staff. *The Fall of a President*. New York: Dell, 1974.

―――. *The Presidential Transcripts*. New York: Dell, 1974.

White, Theodore H. *Breach of Faith*. New York: Atheneum, 1975.

―――. *The Making of the President, 1960*. New York: Atheneum, 1961.

―――. *The Making of the President, 1964*. New York: Atheneum, 1965.

―――. *The Making of the President, 1968*. New York: Atheneum, 1969.

―――. *The Making of the President, 1972*. New York: Atheneum, 1973.

Wills, Gary. *Nixon Agonistes*. New York: Houghton Mifflin, 1971.

Woodward, Bob, and Bernstein, Carl. *All the President's Men*. New York: Simon and Schuster, 1974.

―――. *The Final Days*. New York: Simon and Schuster, 1976.

INDEX

289

C

Hoyt, Palmer, 85
Hughes, Howard, 99–100
Humphrey, Hubert H., 24–25, 112–13, 117, 118, 122–23
Hungate, William, 242–43
Hunt, Dorothy, 169–70; death of, 175–76
Hunt, E. Howard, 123, 135–49, 152–57, 159, 166; pay-off demands of, 169–72, 177, 189–91, 222; trial, 168, 176–77, 194–95
Hurley, Patrick S.,35–36
Hutchinson, Edward, 232

Illinois politics, 25–30
impeachment, 219–20, 230–56; definition of, 228–29
incumbent candidates, 271
independent candidates, 271
Inouye, Daniel, 187
Israel, 116, 180–81

J

Jackson, Andrew, 21
Jackson, Henry (Scoop), 93, 95, 117

Jaworski, Leon, 13, 221, 225–26, 227, 230, 234–35, 237, 238, 243
Jefferson, Thomas, 19–20, 69, 70
Jefferson County, Kentucky, 38
Jenkins, Walter, 78–80
Johnson, Andrew, 228
Johnson, Lyndon Baines, 3–17, 25, 50, 58–59, 61, 65, 78–82, 86–88
Jones, Thomas V., 171

Kalmbach, Herbert W., 114, 169–72
Kansas City politics, 30–31
Kelly, Douglas, 114–15, 117–19
Kennedy, Edward M., 184
Kennedy, John F., 15, 24–27, 55–67, 112
Kennedy, Joseph P., 24
Kennedy, Robert F., 61
Kentucky politics, 38, 109
Kissinger, Henry, 255
Kleindienst, Richard, 151–52, 200–202, 206
Ku Klux Klan, 22, 62–63

T

U